T10848

B
Jor

Jordan, Ruth

Daughter of the Waves: Memories
of Growing Up in Pre-War
Palestine

DEMCO

Daughter of the Waves

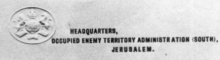

30. 6. 20.

Handed over to Sir Herbert Samuel, one Palestine, complete —

L. J. Bols.
Major General.

From occupied territory into British Mandate. This document, dated June 30, 1920, and signed by Major General L. J. Bols, reads: "Handed over to Sir Herbert Samuel, one Palestine, complete."
(Courtesy Israel State Archives)

Daughter of the Waves

Memories of Growing Up in Pre-War Palestine

by **Ruth Jordan**

Taplinger Publishing Company
New York

B
Jor
T/0848

First printing
Published in 1983 by
TAPLINGER PUBLISHING CO., INC.
New York, New York

LIBRARY OF CONGRESS CATALOGING IN PUBLICATION DATA

Jordan Ruth.
    Daughter of the Waves.
    1. Jordan, Ruth.   2. Jews in Palestine—Biography.
3. Palestine—Biography.   I. Title.
CT1919.P38J674   956.94'04'0924 [B]   80-39526
ISBN 0-8008-2120-3

For Sharon and Oran

Contents

Acknowledgments   9

Foreword   11

PART ONE: *Innocence*   13
    1. Earliest Memories   15
    2. Roots   23
    3. Daughter of the Waves   35
    4. Reality and Fantasy   45
    5. Finding Out   51
    6. Hadar Hacarmel   61
    7. The Battle of the Languages 69
    8. School   75

PART TWO: *A New World*   89
    9. First Glimpse of the Palestine Triangle 91
    10. British and American   101
    11. Bo-Kah   113
    12. Buy Hebrew   123
    13. Music Ho!   133
    14. The Great Years   141
    15. A Taste of Adventure   153
    16. Back at Bat Galim   161
    17. Toscanini   175

PART THREE: *Days of Wrath*   185
    18. Doing My Bit   187
    19. Flare-up   197
    20. Epilogue   209

Acknowledgments

I AM INDEBTED to my sister Yardena, my brother Gideon, and my childhood friend Zephyra for helping me to unlock from subconsciousness impressions and memories which have been overlaid by later experiences. I am grateful to photographers Rachel Hirsch of Tel Aviv and Moshe Friedman of Jerusalem for making the most of yellowing snapshots found in family albums, and to the following for putting at my disposal historical photographs, some of which have never been published before: the Israel State Archives and the Jewish National Fund Picture Collection in Jerusalem; the Hagana Archives, the Israel Philharmonic Orchestra Archives and the Central Library of Music and Dance in Tel Aviv; Mrs. Zivia Halutz and the late Mrs. Miriam Bourla; and the Public Relations Department of the Furness Withy Shipping Group in London. Finally, as ever, my warmest thanks to my family for their interest and encouragement.

Foreword

WHEN THE FIRST WORLD WAR was over the newly established
League of Nations entrusted Great Britain with a mandate
to govern Palestine, which she did until 1948. I was born in
Haifa during the first decade of the mandate and lived most
of my childhood and adolescence in a seaside suburb called
Bat Galim, Daughter of the Waves, before leaving for England at the beginning of 1946.

In setting down my youthful recollections my aim is not
to retell the political events of the period—except when
such retelling helps to clarify the narrative—but to describe how ordinary people lived their everyday life during those early years of national development. As I remember it, life in mandatory Palestine of the 1920s and
the 1930s was not all violence and White Papers. It was
indolently pleasant, as only life in a Mediterranean cli-
mate can be, and with it excitingly active, as only life in a
dedicated national community can be.

Most of the people I knew as a child were not involved
with politics; yet, because their very being in Palestine was
a fulfillment of an ideal, everything they did or said tran-
scended the personal and took on a national significance.
Even such private ventures as building a house on the
seafront, opening a European-style café, or exploring historic sites contributed in their way to the making of a
homeland and the shaping of its economy, culture, and
mores. Palestine was an intimate society where everybody
knew everybody. In 1908, when my parents met and mar-

ried in Haifa, the total Jewish population of the country was about 60,000; in the mid-twenties, when my recollections begin, it was 108,000; and in 1939, when they end, it was just over 400,000.

Childhood memories are like flashes of lightning; visions of people, animals, and events without beginning or end, appearing and disappearing with no explanation asked for or offered. Only gradual awareness puts the fragments into perspective and knits disjointed sequences into a coherent pattern. In retrospect I see that if the experiences of my early life were entirely personal, their broad outline was common enough among those of my generation. I absorbed the ideals, as well as the prejudices, of my social and ethnic environment. I grew up, like so many of my contemporaries, idealistic as well as cynical, naive as well as distrustful, proud of my heritage as well as irresistibly drawn to an unknown cultural world called Europe. I took for granted that the country of my birth would always be as I found it, a national home for the Jews, sometimes tolerated but more often attacked by the native Arabs who were, however, as much part of it as the hills and the sea.

Daughter of the Waves does not attempt to judge or analyze, justify or apologize. It is a look back at a cherished landscape, a record of the impressions and experiences of one who grew up in the emotional security of a homeland against a background of different cultures, mentalities, and customs. Above all, it is a memorial to a vanished era which has left its mark on present-day attitudes, fears, and hopes.

London 1980

PART
ONE
Innocence

I remember, I remember
The house where I was born,
The little window where the sun
Came peeping in the morn;
He never came a wink too soon
Nor brought too long a day . . .

Thomas Hood, 1799–1845

I

Earliest Memories

IT WAS SUMMER.

It was always summer when I was a child. When I opened my eyes in the morning, the sun was already shining bright, tracing its daily semicircle over the sky before sinking into the sea. In the evening I watched it set from the veranda of our tamarisk-surrounded house on the beach, straining my eyes to catch the precise moment when the flame-red horizon would begin to dim and change into melancholy gray. Sunset in Haifa, as in all Mediterranean regions, was followed by instant night. One moment the sun would loom large over the sea and flood it with its lengthening rays; the next it would be swallowed up to allow impudent little stars to assert themselves against a rapidly darkening sky.

It was summer; and perhaps it was also a Saturday, for my father was off work and my brother off school. The three of us had set out on a day's hike to the Mound of Shikmona, some two miles south of Haifa, which my father said had once been a Roman fortress. Father was wearing his tropical khaki helmet, as integral a part of his person as his short black beard. He was carrying sandwiches in a rucksack and water in an old army canteen. My ten-year-old brother was also carrying a canteen slung over his shoulder, while I was allowed to toddle behind unburdened. It must have been 1926.

We were following a rough road meandering between

the weedy coast on the right and the low hills of the Carmel range on the left. The road was deserted. There were no Arab peasant women balancing bundles of twigs on their heads, no line of donkeys with illegally quarried sand in their saddlebags, not even the occasional donkey rider followed on foot by an obedient wife. A small Arab village nestled against the mountain slope, its few houses painted light blue against the evil eye. It was hot. It was so hot that even the ill-tempered village dogs could not be bothered to chase us and contented themselves with a perfunctory bark from a distance.

The sound of iron-shod wheels rolling against the rough road made us look back and quickly make way for a mule-drawn cart driven by an Arab villager. As he overtook us he slowed down, and I noticed the dazzling white of his *kaffiye* held to his head by the black *agal*.

"Let your day be happy," father called to the driver.

"Let yours be blessed," the driver answered, not the least bit surprised to be addressed in his own language by a European Jew.

There followed an exchange of civilities based on a time-honored code which my father had learned in his childhood from his Arab playmates near the village of Zichron Yaakov. It was quite a while before the two men felt it was correct to set formalities aside and embark on an ordinary conversation.

There was an oblong black box on the cart, which the driver said he was taking to a nearby village for somebody's funeral. As he was explaining his errand, holding back his mule to allow us to keep pace with him, his eyes lighted on me, panting heavily behind two grown men. He pulled at the reins, and the mule stopped.

"She's slowing you down," he said.

I was intrigued. Only a few days earlier I had heard our Arab washerwoman tell how her little niece had been promised in marriage to a little boy from a neighboring village for a sackful of grain. At the time I thought it was a silly exchange, but now I was wondering whether the cart driver was trying to buy me for his son. Speaking disparagingly of the object one wished to purchase, I already knew, was the best way to lower its price.

"She's slow," the cart driver repeated. "Slow."

Father said it did not matter as we were in no hurry.

"*Ma'alesh*, never mind," the cart driver cried good humoredly. "She can ride with me on the box."

It was kindness, not an attempt to buy me. I was lifted and seated on top of the coffin with my back to the driver and my feet dangling down, free to enjoy a bumpy ride while my father and brother kept pace behind. We parted company at the foot of Shikmona Mound, my father calling on Allah to reward our benefactor sevenfold for his kindness, our benefactor wishing the blessing of Allah upon my father, his sons, his cattle, and his house.

The mound looked like any other hill; excavations had not yet been thought of. It was covered with mean little shrubs and I wondered how the Roman legionaries could have hidden among them. Later I picked up a torso-shaped piece of blue glass washed smooth by the waves and claimed an archaeological find. My father earnestly explained that although it was not likely to be Roman, it could well be a piece of refuse from a ruined glass factory established nearby by Baron Edmond de Rothschild in 1891.

The word Baron, pronounced in Hebrew with the stress on the last syllable, made a deep impression. I imagined a black-haired man striding masterfully along the sand dunes, pointing his wand to spots where he desired glass palaces to be put up. At home the piece of glass was placed on a shelf next to my two other treasures, a ginger-colored sweet shaped like a cat, and one-half of an empty Christmas cracker.

The Christmas cracker had first belonged to Naomi and

Nigel Holmes, who lived in a large house next to ours. I knew their father as Mr. Holmes-the-Haifa-manager-of-the-Palestine-Railways, although that may not have been his official designation. There was a Mrs. Holmes somewhere in the background and a Sudanese chauffeur in a long white robe who lived in the lodge. I liked sidling along the high wall which separated the Holmes's garden from ours and sniffing my fill of the strange cooking smells which wafted from the lodge. Sometimes I climbed over and went into the house to play with Naomi and Nigel. I never used the gate.

It was a mysterious house, full of dark brown doors, rambling wooden staircases, and strange pieces of furniture which, so Naomi and Nigel proudly told me, had come from England. They had the most exciting toys. There was a scooter which was much more fun than my own tricycle, and a dark brown box called a gramophone which could be made to sing "Baa Baa Black Sheep" and "Humpty-Dumpty." For some reason the gramophone had been placed on a high shelf and whenever we wanted to use it we had to climb a wardrobe to reach it. Once when it was my turn to climb up I accidentally pushed the tone arm and we thought I had broken it. The children rushed upstairs to fetch their father while I stayed fearfully perched on top of the wardrobe awaiting my doom. But Mr. Holmes, a gentle giant, reached up to the gramophone with one hand, put things right, and told me to climb down. Then he rummaged in a chest of drawers and offered me a small cylinder wrapped in crepe paper and neatly tied at both ends.

"A Christmas cracker," Naomi and Nigel gasped simultaneously. "But it's summer!"

I had never seen a Christmas cracker before and did not understand why it was unusual to see one in summer. Naomi and Nigel began saying a whole lot of silly things, talking about lights in trees and something called snow, which they said was like the block of ice in the icebox, only it wasn't because it was soft. They showed me how to pull the ends and I liked the detonation and the delicate whiff of gunpowder. When we saw the Sudanese chauffeur drive Mr. Holmes out, we rummaged in the chest of drawers until we found, and pulled, two more Christmas crackers.

My other cherished possession, the ginger-colored sweet shaped like a cat, was also a present from the Holmses. Its shape and color were unique, for ordinary sweets were round and red. Usually they were bought at the Bat Galim general store from the formidable Mr. Milles. You handed him your precious copper coin of two millimes and pointed wordlessly to a large glass jar half filled with unwrapped, sticky sweets. Mr. Milles would put away the coin, thrust his forearm into the jar, and scoop up a handful; then, without weighing it, he would drop the mess into a paper cornet and push it across the counter. Afterwards it was difficult to pull out a sweet without bits of gray paper sticking to it. By contrast, my cat-sweet was hard and smooth and did not melt even in the height of summer. It was altogether too good to be eaten. I was convinced that the Holmses had brought it over from England together with their gramophone and Christmas crackers, but today I suspect that they bought it at Spinney's, a well-appointed store in the German Colony, which specialized in British-made tinned food and confectionery.

The visit to Shikmona was followed by an outing to a remote part of Mount Carmel called the Trees of the Forty. Father was a great organizer of such outings. He had got in touch with a local bus driver who went by the name of Ivan the Proselyte and hired him and his vehicle for a certain Saturday. Word went around Bat Galim that a visit to an historic site was being arranged, and the sleepy suburb buzzed with excitement. For many families it was their first chance to explore the Carmel range, and they hastened to enroll with devotional zeal kindled by a patriotic urge to get to know the ancient homeland.

Ivan's bus could take us only as far as the Druze village of Ussufiye; from there on we followed a donkey trail through a shady oak forest until we reached a clearing bounded on one side by an imposing rock. This was our destination. Father explained that the Forty, after whom the forest was called, were holy men who sought God among the trees. Muslim tradition had it that their spirits still hovered about the place. Strips of white cloth tied to the branches proclaimed the oak trees to be sacred, and a recess in the rock served as a shrine. Nonbelievers were unwelcome in such a holy place and a number of Arab youths hung about to see what the infidel *yahud* were up to, watching sullenly as picnic baskets were unpacked, canteens passed from hand to hand, and litter scrupulously collected. I picked up a greenish stone the size and shape of a coconut and took it to my brother.

"Dad," he cried excitedly, "she's found an Elijah watermelon."

No outing was ever complete without a talk on the history and folklore of the place visited, and my find gave father a further opportunity to link the present with the past. The Book of Kings, he explained, tells us that when Elijah the Tishbite went into hiding in the ravine of Kerith east of the river Jordan, God appointed two ravens to bring him bread and meat morning and evening. No such provision was made for the prophet when he wandered about Mount Carmel to escape the long hand of the followers of Baal; Arab tradition had it that he lived on scraps begged from local peasants. One day, my father continued, Elijah passed by a field of watermelons and wondered whether he could have one. A peasant was sitting cross-legged in the watchtower, a wooden platform on stilts with a sack awning to protect him from the heat of the sun.

"God be with you," Elijah called to the peasant. "May I pick one of your lovely watermelons to quench my thirst?"

"Watermelons?" the peasant called back. "I don't see any watermelons. Those things in the field are stones."

"May God grant that you have been speaking the truth," Elijah shouted angrily.

At that moment all the lovely watermelons turned into stones, and some of them, my father concluded gravely, may still be found on Mount Carmel.

Elijah was the local patron prophet. The Arabs called him *al chader*, the Green Man, and had faith in his healing powers. Father once led a hike to a shrine called Elijah's Cave on the lower slopes of the mountain just outside Bat Galim, where Arabs as well as oriental Jews often came to light candles, make wishes, and fulfill vows. A visit to the cave was particularly recommended, father told the young women in the party, for wives who wanted to have a male baby. All they had to do was to spend three days and nights there alone.

2

Roots

As a child I took it for granted that life for other people began, as it did for me, the day I was born. Things which happened earlier were beyond my grasp. Mother and father, even my sister and brother, seemed to have lived in a dark tunnel from which they emerged only when I began to observe, feel, and experience for myself. I therefore took in little of what my parents told me of their own lives, and it was only after their deaths that I came to reconstruct the history and background of their respective families.

Father was a third-generation native of Palestine, born in the village of Zichron Yaakov near Haifa in 1886 or 1887. There was no certainty, not even in his parents' minds, about his exact date of birth since the registration of births under Ottoman rule was usually carried out long after the event and was often haphazard and imprecise.

His ancestors had lived in Moravia, which had a small Jewish community since the eleventh century. Some of them had dealt in grain and flour; others kept a cow or two until an edict issued in 1804 forbade Jews to buy cattle for any purpose other than slaughter. In 1820 or thereabouts my great-great-grandfather, then in his twenties, left Moravia for Palestine with a view to keeping cows in a land flowing with milk and honey. The Land of Milk and Honey, it will be recalled, had been under Ottoman rule since 1517 and was to remain so until the middle of the First World War.

The young man made straight for Jerusalem. In those

days the custom was, as indeed it still is, for visitors to the Western Wall to write their requests to God on a tiny slip of paper and push it, neatly folded, in between the cracks of the massive stones. My great-great-grandfather did the same, then turned his thoughts to the pressing matter of finding himself a wife.

Most of the Jewish community of the Holy City lived in squalor, but their womenfolk bloomed in penury like the pink flowers in the cracks of the Western Wall. They were noted for their fair complexion and vivacity, and what they lacked by way of dowry they made up for in hard work. My great-great-grandfather, a poor young man himself, took a bride who was as sturdy as she was fair. There is no evidence that the young couple ever kept cows, or even a single goat, but a grandson of theirs called Elazar—to me Grandfather Elazar—was among the original settlers of Zichron Yaakov, a village established in 1882 by Baron Edmond de Rothschild on the slopes of Mount Carmel.

Grandfather Elazar brought with him his newly wedded wife, another sturdy Jerusalemite, who gave him a daughter and five sons, of whom my father was one. For fourteen years Elazar worked in the vines which were to make Zichron Yaakov famous but, like so many of the original settlers, he was disenchanted with the baronial administration. In 1896 he took his large family to a remote valley near the Lebanese border to found the village of Metulla. Although Metulla was established with Rothschild funds, the settlers had been promised greater freedom from baronial control.

Metulla's development followed the familiar pattern of Arab attacks and Jewish self-defense. The land handed over to the settlers had been legally—and expensively—purchased by the Rothschild agency, but while the wealthy Arab landlord went to live on his other property elsewhere, the native peasants who had been tilling his fields on a feudal system and living in tied mud huts had nowhere to go to. When told to clear out they felt dispossessed. They departed full of hate, not for the uncaring *effendi* who had sold them off his land, but for the foreigners who had bought it from him. Some tried to win back by force the huts and fields they had considered theirs, and nighttime attacks were not infrequent. Grandfather Elazar built his stone farmhouse on a high plateau overlooking a Lebanese valley, with firing slits in the back wall. The house still stands, its outside scarred with bullet holes left by generations of snipers.

While Grandfather Elazar was planting plum trees and apple trees in the fertile soil of Upper Galilee, my father, who was then about ten, looked after a pomegranate tree he had found growing near the new farmhouse. He tended it carefully, examined it daily, and marveled at its budding red bloom. He had never seen a pomegranate flower before. He guarded it jealously from covetous friends and was anxious if anybody as much as looked at it. He was in love with it.

One night he woke up with a start and rushed out to discover a Druze boy of about his own age standing under the tree. The precious bloom had not been harmed. The two boys stared at each other in the faint moonlight, unfrightened and hostile, until the young Druze broke the silence.

"My mother rocked my cradle under this tree," he whispered fiercely. "My father planted it for me. You have driven us out of our home."

The Jewish boy knew instinctively that only a tremendous act of renunciation could soothe the Druze boy's sense of injury. With a dying heart he reached for the pomegranate flower and plucked it with one sharp twist. "Take it," he said. "It's yours."

The Druze boy hesitated for a moment, then snatched the flower and vanished into the night.

The years spent in Metulla were among the most formative in my father's life. He often played truant from school in order to climb a hill, follow an unexplored path, or descend into a Druze village. The scenery was extraordinary. The Naphtali range of mountains rose in the west, the Golan Heights towered over the village from the east, and the snow-capped Mount Hermon gleamed from afar in all seasons. There was the shimmering beauty of a water cascade locally known as the Chimney, and the lush vegetation by the never-drying springs fed by rainwater and melting snow from Mount Hermon. Father walked to Tel-El-Kadi to see the river Dan, one of the sources of the Jordan, and ventured into foreign territory to see the two other sources, the Hasbani and the Banias. Already a fluent Arabic speaker since his early encounters with the young lads of Zamarin, the Arab village near his native Zichron Yaakov, he now learned from his new Druze friends some of the rich Arabic vocabulary of civility, good manners, and social etiquette.

At the small Metulla school he spoke nothing but Hebrew. While learning from his father how to mend a plow, prune fruit trees, and trail mules stolen by neighboring Arabs, he delved into Mishnaic literature to retrieve the correct Hebrew words to describe those time-honored agricultural tasks which the settlers were just rediscovering. His instinct for etymology and linguistic purity informed his speech and writing to the end of his life.

He was about fourteen when he was sent to the agricultural school of Mikve Israel, founded in 1870 by a French Jewish organization called *Alliance Israélite Universelle.* There he acquired enough French to win a grant to the University of Grenoble to complete his agricultural studies. On his return he realized that the Metulla farm was too small to support parents, five grown sons, and a daughter, and decided to change course. He went to Haifa, which at that time was an Arab town with a Jewish population of less than a thousand, and started its first secular Hebrew school. He named it *Avtalia,* Father of the Lamb, implying that he would treat the kids in his charge like a father. After a while he engaged an assistant, a young woman who had just arrived from Europe with an impressive record of teaching behind her.

The young woman, who was to become my mother, was born in 1880 in Vilna, Lithuania, and while still a baby was moved to Warsaw. Her father manufactured and sold boots, but the children were never allowed to forget that he came from a long line of rabbinical scholars. The family lived comfortably. There were maids, silver and cut glass, summer holidays in the country. There were also visiting tutors for the three children. One was a *melamed,* the traditional religion teacher who taught boys their prayer-book Hebrew and coached them for their bar mitzvah ritual at the synagogue. At the age of eight my mother was allowed to join her younger brother in his Hebrew lessons and did far better than he. Gradually she acquired a solid literary foundation in the language, which was to be reflected in her beautiful everyday speech when she settled in Palestine.

Other tutors who called at the house coached the children for the entrance examination to the Warsaw Russian Gymnasium. Because of the *Numerus Clausus,* an official restriction on the number of Jewish pupils admitted to state institutions of education, competition among Jewish applicants was keen. After mother was accepted she kept up a remarkable record. She was a born linguist and, apart from the Yiddish and Hebrew learned at home, she mastered Russian, German, and French, not to mention school Latin. She sketched, played the piano, and carried off the school prize in mathematics. Her math master suggested that she should continue her studies abroad, but her father pronounced that a university was no place for a decent Jewish girl. Mother began teaching and saved up. At the age of twenty-two, quietly defying parental authority, she left for Geneva to study for a degree in natural history. It was 1902.

In Geneva she joined a society of Jewish students whose imagination had been fired by the age-old dream of returning to Zion. The World Zionist Organization had been founded only a few years earlier, and the term Zionism, a made-up word to replace the original but rather cumbersome *Hibat Zion*, Love of Zion, had only just entered world vocabulary. Mother taught Hebrew and attended Zionist meetings. There was a young science researcher at the university, a lecturer in organic chemistry, who sometimes spoke at those meetings and was listened to with great interest. He was Dr. Hayim Weizmann, later Israel's first president, then still in his twenties.

After she had obtained her degree mother returned to Warsaw and ordered a supply of visiting cards with the words *Miriam Raphelkes, Bachelier ès sciences naturelles, Varsovie*. The surname Raphelkes had been adopted by an ancestor who lived opposite the church of St. Raphael, but mother's friends addressed her as Mlle Marie or, more familiarly, Mania. She was short, with a fair complexion and light brown hair braided around her head after the fashion of the day. Her best feature was her gray-blue eyes which turned pure blue whenever she was excited or out of breath. She was vain about them and once told me how, when she was about to have her first passport issued in Warsaw, she ran twice round the block to make herself breathless, and her eyes bluer, before presenting herself to the scrutiny of the passport clerk.

She lived at home and went out to teach and attend Zionist meetings. Before long she became headmistress of a girls' school called *Yehudia*, the Jewess. In 1905 she went to Basel to attend the seventh Zionist Congress, and in 1907 she went to the Hague to attend the eighth. Her activities were considered subversive and her movements were closely watched. When she was tipped off one night that she was about to be arrested, she hid in the undergrowth of a neighboring garden and made a dash for a Geneva-bound train just before daybreak. She never saw Warsaw again. As soon as mother reached safety she began to arrange for her passage to Palestine. Thirty years later, when I asked her what her strongest motive for going to Palestine had been, she answered with vehemence: "I wanted a homeland. I was not going to settle down and give birth to children in a country where they would one day be persecuted. I wanted them to be born in a country they would have a right to call their own."

And so she returned to ancient Zion. In 1908 she disembarked at the port of Jaffa complete with hat, veil, gloves, and a long trailing skirt. Jaffa in those days was the only Palestinian port where ships could call with any degree of safety, but since the natural curve of the coast had not yet been assisted by a man-made harbor or breakwater, the ships had to anchor in the open sea. The arrival of a ship was a great event. As soon as it came into view the sleepy Arab boatmen jumped into their boats and rowed towards it to ferry back passengers and luggage. Ferocious-looking porters in black baggy breeches rushed up the gangway yelling at the top of their voices, snatched and dumped trunks into the boats, shouted at the bemused passengers, and flung them unceremoniously into the boats after their luggage. Mother shouted back in every language she knew but their own; later she picked up colloquial Arabic from a string of washerwomen, fishermen, and vegetable vendors.

On the day of her disembarkation the sea was relatively calm; even so the waves broke against the sides of the boat and flooded it with water and sea foam. The women screamed, the men shouted advice, the oarsmen yelled at each other in their guttural voices, and a small Arab boy bailed water with a rusty tin can. The current was carrying them towards an ominous black rock and for a moment it looked as if they were all going to be smashed against it. Local legend had it, mother later heard, that storms were stirred up by a fierce sea monster clamoring for a human sacrifice. The only way to appease him was to offer him an unsullied maiden. Many generations earlier, long before living memory, a beautiful princess was left tied to the rock as a peace offering for the monster, but before he had a chance to claim her a young prince named Perseus came flying on his winged horse and rescued her. When my mother first saw it, the massive basalt was still known as the Rock of Andromeda.

Mother stayed in Jaffa—Tel Aviv had not yet come into being—just long enough to admire the Herzlia Gymnasium recently launched by the thriving Jewish community of the town. Then she left for Haifa, with its much smaller Jewish community, to teach at its first Hebrew school.

Avtalia School was housed in an Arab-owned building in the German Colony and consisted of some twenty boys and girls of various ages. Mother taught reading and writing, sums, and singing while the headmaster, who was the only other teacher, taught botany, geography, and the stories of the Bible. The native-born headmaster took it upon himself to guide his blue-eyed assistant, city bred and sophisticated as she was, on long walks up Mount Carmel and instill in her his own fervent love for every rock, clump of trees, and dried-up stream. In winter they climbed hills dotted with conifers, at springtime they walked over wild stretches covered with golden gorse, red anemones, pink cyclamen, white crocuses, and blue cornflowers. Mother's guide knew the history of every hill and valley. He had a prophet-like turn of phrase, raven black hair, an olive complexion, and gray-green eyes. Before long they were married. Mother was twenty-nine at the time, father about twenty-three. When my sister, their first child, was born, a note was pinned to the school front door: "Closed today on account of Madam's indisposition."

Shortly after my sister's birth father left for Berlin to study biology, leaving mother behind to teach and bring up the baby. In 1911 he visited St. Petersburg where mother's young brother was studying law. "Pinhas's exotic looks are the sensation of St. Petersburg," the brother candidly reported. Mother promptly bundled up her clothes and the baby and rejoined her husband in Berlin. The three of them returned to Haifa just before the outbreak of the First World War, chiefly, as I later often heard, because mother had foreseen its coming and insisted that in times of trouble it was best to be home.

The war years were harsh. Turkey and her allies used Palestine as a base for their assault on Egypt and the Suez Canal, and the inhabitants were required to provide supplies for the 4th Turkish Corps. There was heavy taxation, compulsory labor on the roads and railroads, confiscation of property, and widespread starvation. There was also a savage felling of trees to supply the Ottoman forces. Nearly a generation later mother pointed to the bare slopes of Mount Carmel and said with sadness in her voice, "The name Carmel is derived from *kerem el*, the Vineyard of God. Look at it now, all stark brown. The Turks hacked down all the trees for firewood."

As the war went on, the Turks introduced conscription among the Ottoman subjects of Palestine, irrespective of religion. When my father heard that the conscripting officers were coming he mounted his horse and disappeared into the wilderness, seeking refuge among his friends in the villages of the Druze. Others were not so lucky. Some were forced to serve in the army of a corrupt regime they wished to be rid of, and some, rightly suspected of spying for Britain, were arrested, sent to Damascus, tortured, and executed.

In 1917 a British force led by General Allenby conquered Palestine, and four hundred years of Ottoman domination came to an end. While the future of the area was debated in political conferences, a British military command was set up under the title of Occupied Enemy Territory Administration (South). The League of Nations later entrusted Great Britain with a mandate to govern the occupied territories on both sides of the river Jordan, and a former cabinet minister, the Jewish Sir Herbert Samuel, was appointed first High Commissioner for Palestine. On June 30, 1920, Major General Bols, the British military governor in charge of OETA (South), relinquished his command with a simple chit of paper: "Handed over to Sir Herbert Samuel, one Palestine, complete." The territory across the Jordan soon became a separate political entity under the name of Trans-Jordan.

The changing fortunes of Palestine were reflected in the original status of each of my parents' three children. My sister was born under the Ottoman regime; my brother was born into a country in transition; I came into the world when Palestine was already a full-fledged British mandatory territory. I was born at the newly opened government hospital in Haifa, and mother was forever telling me how alarmed the young English doctor at the maternity ward was when he realized that the pregnant woman before him was in her forties. As it happened, that late and last of her confinements was also the easiest. She wanted to call me Ariel, but the rest of the family decided otherwise.

By the time my recollections begin my mother was graying and my father was teaching natural history at the Haifa Reali School, which had superseded Avtalia. His zeal for his subject was such that he thought nothing of walking six miles each way to look at an unusual plant or follow the dry bed of an unidentified mountain stream. He founded the Palestine Ramblers Association and walked with them the width and breadth of Palestine and Trans-Jordan, entered the Sinai desert through Egypt and sketched innumerable maps of uncharted terrains. His name became synonymous with a patriotic leisure activity called Knowledge of the Country.

3

Daughter of the Waves

WE LIVED IN A RESIDENTIAL SUBURB by the sea, which my father, being one of the founders, had named *Bat Galim*, Daughter of the Waves. It consisted of bungalows and houses, each on its own grounds planted with tamarisks, palms, fig trees, and bougainvillea. Attempts to grow carnations and irises in the sandy soil had to be abandoned. There were no proper roads, but romantic names had been given to stretches of sand which were scheduled to be surfaced one day with a mixture of gravel and pitch. A sand dune outside our front gate was called Seagull Road while another dune encroaching on a side gate was called Azure Street. At the back, behind a pit of black soil, ran Vineyard Lane. I never saw a single vine growing in the sand. The vineyards and the fields, all cultivated by neighboring Arabs, were well away from the sand dunes, hugging the slopes of the fertile Carmel range.

Before they moved to Bat Galim in 1923, my family had been living in a rented house in the German Colony, founded in Haifa in the second half of the nineteenth century by a contingent of German Knights Templars. It was a quiet, respectable suburb, with solid houses and tidy front gardens where tomato plants were trained to grow around tall cypresses. The move from the civilized German Colony to the virgin sand dunes by the sea was the idea of a group of professional people who had had enough of living in congested rented accommodations and wanted to own their own house and garden. They bought the land jointly from its Arab and German owners, divided it up, and started building. Mother had sold her collection of indoor plants for ten Egyptian pounds—the currency of the day—in order to put down the initial deposit on the building site.

There was no architectural master plan, and each family designed its house according to its own needs and tastes. Ours had a large living room opening onto a veranda which overlooked the sea. Only fifty yards or so separated the house from the water's edge. During the winter, when the sea was rough, the waves broke over the garden wall, flooding the veranda and seeping under the door into the living room. The ground floor also had two bedrooms, a kitchen with another veranda, amenities, and a box room which had been intended for a maid, only we never had one. The bedroom ceilings were fitted with iron hooks from which mosquito nets dangled loosely. When the nets became too tatty to serve any useful purpose they were discarded and never replaced; we were none the worse for it.

Upstairs there were two more bedrooms leading to a large flat roof. Once I encountered a tall lady dressed in black coming down the stairs. I knew she was my grandmother but I had nothing to say to her. When she had gone the rooms were taken over by a mysterious German scientist who carried out experiments on the flat roof. He used to take his midday meal with us, and it was my duty to knock on his door and call him down.

"Kommen Sie essen, Herr Steinitz," I would say, peeping into his rooms. He never corrected my faulty German.

One day, as Herr Steinitz made to go downstairs, I squeezed myself flat against the banister to let him pass, then sneaked up to inspect his rooms. There were books, a microscope, a panama hat, and several wicker-covered bottles, larger than any I had ever seen. The bottles were empty and had a strong unfamiliar smell. On the flat roof there were two wicker cases which begged to be explored; when I unlocked them they revealed more wicker-covered bottles, all rotund, unopened, and heavy. Mother later explained that Dr. Steinitz was an important gentleman who had to have a constant supply of German beer at hand to help him with his experiments. What the experiments were I could not make out. One evening I heard him call my father with great excitment from the top of the staircase: *"Herr Doktor, Herr Doktor, Kommen Sie schnell!"*

My father was no *Herr Doktor*, but Dr. Steinitz must have felt it was the proper way to address a master of biology at a highly academic school.

"What's up?" my father shouted back.

"It's the amoeba. Come and look."

Father leaped up the stairs two at a time. Shortly the two men shouted for mother to come up and take a look at the slides. When Dr. Steinitz left us to return to his native Germany he bequeathed—or sold—his microscope to father, along with some slides. One evening father put the microscope on the rough round table on the living-room veranda and told me to close one eye and look. The slides had been tinted red to reveal the shapes of some peculiar-looking creatures. Father said that Dr. Steinitz had made a great contribution to Mediterranean marine biology. I did not understand what marine biology was, but I knew it had something to do with wicker baskets and demijohns of beer.

A typical Bat Galim day started at five in the morning with the arrival of Ahmed from the nearby Arab village. His task was to pump water from the garden well into the storage tank on the top landing. There was no central water supply at Bat Galim, and each house had its own well and hand pump. The water tasted slightly salty and when not used for tea or coffee had to be mixed with red Zichron Yaakov wine to make it drinkable. Sometimes our water consumption for house and garden exceeded the capacity of the tank and made the taps run dry. It was then up to us children to work the pump and refill the storage tank. Ahmed did a hundred strokes each morning before going on to the next house along the sea front to do the same; my brother could do forty; I could do nine or ten.

When Ahmed departed, it was time to stir. Wearing a white sleeveless nightie barely covering my bottom, I would get a tin bowl from the kitchen and run barefoot to the only fig tree in the garden. Picking figs for breakfast required expertise. If the figs had split open to reveal their pretty pink inside, they were over-ripe and not fit for eating. If they were whole and hard they were probably unripe and would bleed a sticky milky sap when plucked. A bowlful of figs which were just right was a daily triumph graciously acknowledged by the entire family. The table on the kitchen veranda was already laid with tomatoes, home-pickled gherkins, home-prepared green olives, bread and butter, and a loaf of salty Safed cheese. There were also soft-boiled eggs, which were either too runny or too hard, and a milky beverage called coffee.

Getting dressed for the day was a simple business. It meant changing from the short nightie into black swimming trunks: no top for flat-chested little girls. Thus dressed, I was ready to help with the daily shopping. It was an agreeable task. All I had to do was rush out to the sand dunes as soon as I heard the familiar trading cries and ask the various Arab vendors to follow me to the kitchen veranda, where mother would do the selecting and haggling.

The yogurt woman was the earliest, and her cry the most musical. She started her walk along the sand dunes at about six in the morning, gracefully balancing a bleached metal pot on her head.

"*Tochdoo laban,*" she chanted.

"*Tochdoo laban,*" I echoed in a low voice. I knew it meant something like "Who will buy my yogurt?" but I did not rush out as quickly as I might have, for I wanted to hear the cry repeated. It was high-pitched, rhythmical, and clear, easily audible above the dull thud of the waves. The woman was tall and slim in her long black robe and smelled of sour milk and oven smoke. When she reached our veranda she put down her pot, uncovered a metal ladle from under her wide belt, and measured out the required quantity into a bowl my mother had provided. The village-made yogurt was sour and unsmooth, and I adored it.

The egg seller was a man of mean appearance, thin, with shifty eyes. "Beyyd, beyyd!" he called out in a rough throaty voice. "Eggs, eggs." He carried them about in a wooden box and handed them to mother one by one, watching her hands as she put them in her rush basket. They were small and covered with chicken muck, but mother said that they were fresher than the cleaner looking eggs imported from Syria and sold at the local general store.

The fisherman, like the yogurt woman, was another creature of grace and beauty. He started his day when the tide was out, and I loved to watch him cast his net right opposite our house. He was dressed in a sleeveless shirt and black billowing breeches which he had pulled up to his knees, baring his muscular legs. The fishing net was tied around his waist. Because the tide was out he had to walk some twenty or thirty yards over the dry, rocky bed of the sea before the water reached his calves. There he stopped, perfectly still, with only a slight tremor in his legs betraying the extent of his effort and concentration. Suddenly, with one swift move, he would release his net and cast it wide into the water. When he pulled it back it was sometimes full of fish, sometimes disappointingly empty.

"Take the fish," I said to him one morning when he had caught his fill, "and follow me."

He took no notice. I realized that although I had started the sentence in Arabic, I had completed it in English. Fortunately the fisherman did not need a half-naked little girl to tell him what to do. On the veranda I witnessed the usual haggling battle. The fisherman named his price knowing full well it would not be accepted, mother gave a contemptuous laugh and offered less than half. The man's voice became querulous, mother's became shrill. At any moment the fisherman might throw his fish back into the net and depart without sale. In the end however, a price acceptable to both parties was reached; the fish, still alive, was put into one of mother's numerous rush baskets, and the fisherman put his money away in a piece of black rag. Then he called on Allah to reward the kind lady for her generosity and mother wished him peace and God's blessing.

Once a fortnight mother went to shop at the Arab market in the Old City. She would first withdraw into her bedroom in her plain shift and floppy sun hat to emerge, a good hour later, with her hair coiled into a bun, her plump figure encased in lace-up stays and a tight fitting dress, her legs covered with silk stockings, and her feet squeezed into town shoes. Thus transformed she would walk through the sands to the local terminal and catch the Arab bus to town. At market a porter would load her boxes of tomatoes, cucumbers, eggs, eggplants, and watermelons on to a *diligence,* the precursor of the modern taxi. It was a luxurious affair, all red plush and white antimacassars, drawn by two horses with beads around their necks. Its arrival at our back gate was an event. There followed a great to-do about the house. Eggs were preserved in empty petrol drums filled with lime water, cucumbers and eggplants were pickled, plums were made into jam, and watermelons were stored in the unoccupied maid's room.

There were usually some ten or twenty watermelons scattered on the cool floor, and at siesta time, when the rest of the world was dead, I would sneak in and lie on them face down, rocking myself forwards and backwards. One afternoon the watermelons acted strangely, rolling independently in all directions and hitting me in the face. The walls of the little room tilted, and the few books on the top shelf came down with a bang. Then everything was still. Mother and father rushed in.

"It was an earthquake," they said.

There were no casualties and no damage in Haifa; the worst of the tremor had been felt in Safed, in Upper Galilee, which had a long history of such disasters. Many years ago, my father said, long before he was born, long before Grandfather Elazar was born, there was a terrible earthquake in Safed, and four thousand Jews were buried alive under the debris. It went down in history as the Great Tremor of 1837.

After my morning chores were over I was free to rush back to the waterfront to do as I pleased. The sea filled my life. At night it lulled me to sleep with the regular heavy thud of the waves barely a stone's throw away; in the morning, as soon as I opened my eyes, its transient calm charmed me out of bed to admire its mirror-smooth surface. The morning, when the sea was out, was the time to walk gingerly over the sharp rocky bed and look closely at tiny crabs and sea anemones. When the tide was in it was best to paddle in a shallow rock pool full of little fishes and smooth stones.

One afternoon father took out the old rowing boat and allowed me to squeeze in with the adults. The sea was choppy and before we had gone very far a vicious wave turned the boat upside down and hurled us all out. I was about to scream that I was drowning when I realized I was afloat. After that I grew bold and ventured out on my own, diving under the waves until I reached the calmer depths far away.

My ambition was to be allowed to go with the gang. This consisted of my brother and some five or six other schoolboys who spent most of their free time defying the waves with improvised seacraft; father's rowing boat had long before disappeared. The boys had hammered together some planks of wood salvaged from a building site and made a raft. Unfortunately it could not carry more than two at a time and capsized whenever the other three or four fought to get on.

One day they came across a boat half buried in the sand along an unfrequented part of the beach. The waves must have washed it out a long time earlier, for it was well entrenched. The boys dug it out, carried it to our back yard, stopped the holes with pitch, painted the outside black and white, and put to sea. Short planks of wood served as oars. My brother appointed himself captain and led daring expeditions into the unknown. Once the boat was past the rocks along the curving coastline I could no longer follow her progress and had to wait for her return with agony in my heart. In the evenings the boys talked excitedly of adventures I had not shared. They called themselves Seawolves. I ached to be a Seawolf too; I begged and nagged, I whined and wailed. It was no use.

One day, however, my brother said in his nonchalant way, "How would you like to come along this afternoon?"

We were squatting on a rock overlooking the sea, watching the sailing boats on the far horizon. There were always two or three about, used by Arab fishermen for deep sea fishing.

"I'm taking the Seawolves out," my brother went on, still scanning the horizon. "We are going to row past the rocks and follow a northward course until we reach the fishermen's landing place. We've never been that far out before."

I could not think of anything to say. I always lost my tongue in moments of excitement but my brother took no notice and went on as if talking to himself.

"The trouble is, the boat isn't up to it."

"Of course she's up to it," I protested loyally. I had found my tongue. "She's marvelous. She skims over the waves like a seagull."

"No she doesn't," my brother said, indifferent to my effusions. "What we want is an oar."

"What about the planks?"

"No good. We want a proper oar. It would make all the difference. Can you imagine how far we could go if we only had a real oar?"

"Where will you get one?"

My brother stopped scanning the horizon and turned his gaze full on me.

"Alexander has got an oar," he said.

I knew very little about Alexander, except that he spoke Polish at home. When he spoke Hebrew his voice had a soft lilt, markedly different from our raucous native notes. It did not sound right. Nothing about him was right; his lanky figure, his pointed chin, his lack of spirits. Nobody liked him much.

Unaccountably, Alexander had an oar. Nobody was more popular than he was when he first took it to the beach; but he was not a natural Seawolf and screamed to turn back when the other boys were keen to ride the waves. After a couple of outings he ceased to appear on the beach, and the boys had to fall back on their makeshift planks. Whenever I passed by his house I could see the beautiful oar in the back yard, dry, forlorn, utterly wasted. It was not right.

"Get Alexander's oar," my brother told me. "Just for the afternoon."

"But . . ."

"There's no but about it. Either you get the oar, or we don't take you in the boat."

And without waiting to hear my anguished wail he jumped down lightly and walked away.

The other Seawolves had already assembled on the beach. They had dragged the boat out of its bedding place behind the rocks and were bailing water, examining fresh holes, selecting makeshift rowing planks.

Suddenly I knew I was about to lose my only chance. I scrambled down the rock and ran as fast as I could to Alexander's house. The oar was in its usual place, unguarded, unwanted. There was no one about. The adults of the household were having their siesta, and Alexander was probably doing the same. I bent down, heaved the oar over my shoulder as I had seen the boys do, and hurried back to the beach. I was desperate to catch them before they put to sea.

The expedition was glorious, full of high waves and unexplored rocks. That night, when oil lamps were glowing in every home, I shouldered my burden once again and stole back to Alexander's house. The family was sitting around a table on the front veranda, enjoying the cool sea breeze. They did not look as if they had missed an oar. I dropped it in the back yard and ran back home.

There were more boating expeditions after that day, though planks of wood had again to make do for oars. The boys continued to tolerate me and grudgingly allowed me to come along whenever one of them had to drop out to run errands for his parents. We did not see much of Alexander, and gradually he faded right out of our lives.

4

Reality and Fantasy

IT WAS STILL SUMMER, or perhaps it was another summer. The tamarisks stood tall and thick between the house and the sands, their evergreen branches damp and salty; a trained eye could discern the tiniest of pink flowers budding on the upper shoots. My father and brother were pointing towards a dark cloud and using a word I had not heard before. Locusts.

The cloud was moving, coming lower, growing larger. Suddenly everything went dark. Another swarm had appeared and was hiding the sun.

"They are descending on the fields," father cried and started running. Other people were also running towards the fields, where the Arab peasants were already trying to drive the pest away by the traditional method of rattling together empty tins to make a frightening din. It was no use. The locusts swooped down on whatever vegetation was in sight, wheat and barley, vines and eggplants, cucumbers and watermelons. The earth, like the sun a few minutes earlier, went dark. The air trembled and reverberated with the beating of empty tins and the sound of munching and crunching, screeching and crackling. The locusts clung fiercely to the greenery and did not let go even when beaten with sticks and spades.

After a while the swarm, hardly diminished, rose and flew in search of fresh pastures. The fields were left black and stark as though devastated by fire. Not a blade of grass had survived, not a leaf on the vines, not even weeds. The peasants picked up hundreds of dead locusts and took them to their mud huts to be fried for supper. There was nothing else to be done. I too picked up a couple and handed them to father to be dissected and examined under the microscope.

Ironically, the only plants which had been spared were the ornamental tamarisks along the seafront; the locusts had not liked their salty taste. Bat Galim owed its tamarisks to Mr. Holmes, the Haifa railway manager, who had brought some cuttings back from the hills of Judea and planted them in his garden. The desert trees adjusted so well to the humid salty sea air that my father too planted a whole row along the front of the house to screen it from the sand and the winds. Soon everybody was planting tamarisks.

My favorite tamarisk was the one behind the kitchen veranda. It had been planted by my brother when I was a baby and I was later told how every day, on his return from school, he pulled it out to see whether it had struck roots. By the time I came to know it the tree was as tall as the first story of the house and had a rusty dustbin underneath it. I liked to visit it when the rest of the household were having their siesta. As soon as I heard the reassuring snores from the main bedroom I would creep out and kneel down by the dustbin. Then I would take off.

The sensation of flying, with my legs folded under me in a kneeling position, was so vivid that even today I find it difficult to accept that I was not actually airborne. Mostly I rose no higher than half the height of the tree, but once or twice I was able to fly all the way up. It was a daily ritual that never failed, but I knew it would work nowhere else except by the dustbin under the tamarisk.

The only witness to that triumph of faith over gravity was Mitzi. She was a ginger cat who looked lean and starved like most of her Mediterranean breed, but was in fact well fed and much petted. She had a way of crawling into a hole in the nursery sofa and taking a nap among the springs and the tufts of kapok. Every time she went in she dug out some more stuffing until the inside of the sofa was like a cavern. One afternoon mother patched the hole with a strong piece of material. That day Mitzi did not turn up for her evening meal. When the following morning she did not turn up for her breakfast either, mother made straight for the sofa, tore off the patch, and put her hand into the hole to retrieve a contentedly entrenched Mitzi with a litter of four.

Pets came and went. One day father biked home from school towing a live snake behind him and was told to keep it in the chicken shed, which was no longer used for its original purpose. When the snake went, there were salamanders in a glass jar. For my third birthday I asked to be bought a goat and was dismayed to hear that it would eat up all the greenery in the garden. I consoled myself with a perky little dog whose name was *Zariz*, the Hebrew for "agile."

Zariz had soft curls the color of sand and a friendly disposition, unlike the fearsome short-bristled mongrels which were known as common or Arab dogs. Most cats and dogs ran wild and did not seem to belong to anybody. When you saw a cat, you threw a stone at it; when you saw a dog, you said *etla'a*, the colloquial Arabic for Go away. If you did not, he was sure to bite.

Long before I could read any of the three official languages of the country, I could recognize the posters on public billboards which carried warnings against rabid dogs in English, Arabic, and Hebrew. The dog catcher was a familiar figure. He was a uniformed Arab, a civil servant from the Public Health Department, who drove around in a horse-drawn van and wielded a lasso with considerable skill. His approach was heralded by a chorus of frantic barking from within the van, where the imprisoned dogs were savaging one another and vainly hurtling themselves against the small barred window.

In a house which during the summer had every door and window wide open it was impossible to keep an eye on Zariz. When he failed to turn up for his shared evening meal with Mitzi, father biked to the Public Health Department in the German Colony and came back to tell us that Zariz was alive, but would have to serve a term in quarantine. There was no word for quarantine in Hebrew, and the way it was pronounced, *karanteena*, made it all the more mystifying. I imagined a glass palace at the bottom of the sea. When forty days later Zariz was released, father bought him a British-made dog collar at Spinney's. A collar, however, was no safe conduct. During the summer months, when the heat could turn even a mild-tempered pet into a ferocious beast, the catcher picked up any dog in sight.

It must have been at about that time that I saw my first film. In the Haifa of the 1920s baby-sitting was unknown and young children tagged behind their parents on social outings even when the day's entertainment was far above their years. Going to the cinema was a popular pastime among adults. The very young were let in with their parents free of charge, while older children were charged only half price. In theory a non-paying toddler was expected to sit on its mother's lap, but mother always managed to spot a vacant row and settle the whole family down without fuss.

The main Haifa cinema was situated in the Arab Old City, a long and adventurous bus ride from Bat Galim. It was an open-air theater planted with banana trees and sheltered from the heat by the back walls of stone houses. There were small tables under the trees, and during the day the *effendis*, the Arab townsmen, sat around them sipping black coffee and smoking bubbling water pipes called *nar-*

guilas. At night the tables were put away, and films were projected across the garden. It was a lovely place which bore the Hebrew name of *Hagan Ha Mesameah*, the Garden that Delights.

Those were the days of silent films. The pianist, a fat lady with her hair in a bun, sat off to the side and pounded away. I often wondered how she could play so much music from memory and how she knew when to make it sad and when to make it gay. On the left of the main screen there was a small oblong one for subtitles written in Hebrew and Arabic. Since I could not yet read, I kept nagging whoever sat next to me to tell me what was going on.

The first silent film I remember was a serialized adaptation of Victor Hugo's *Les Misérables*. We went to the Garden that Delights on three consecutive weeks to see it through. *Die Nibelungen* was another such serialization. I found it difficult to follow even with the whispered commentary, and when back home I pestered mother, father, sister, and brother to tell me what it had been all about. I was impressed, however, by the sight of Siegfried bathing in the dragon's blood by a forest stream, with a strong wind getting up and a fallen leaf sticking to his back, leaving it vulnerable to Hagen's spear. I hated Hagen and thought Siegfried beautiful with his curly wet hair.

Some time after I had been to see *Die Nibelungen* I saw a new boy playing on the seafront and exclaimed delightedly, "Siegfried!"

He was slim with lovely soft curls on his head, not too long and not too short. He had to be Siegfried.

His father was a doctor newly arrived from Germany. When they came to call, I ran excitedly to mother: "Siegfried is here!"

And Siegfried he remained, even when we grew up and his beautiful curls were shorn and the legend of the Nibelungs became associated with Wagner and anti-Semitism.

The Garden that Delights was in due course supplanted by a film theater with a proper auditorium, projection room, screen, and fixed rows of chairs. It was also situated in the Old City. One evening we sat in the sweltering heat, cracking sunflower seeds and spitting the shells onto the floor as was the custom. The hero of the film had just commandeered a car and ordered the driver to give chase. As the car was speeding towards us, there was a crash and bang from the back stalls. Some Arab peasants, who had never been to a cinema before, thought that the car was going to run them over. They had jumped out of their seats, pushing the entire row backwards, and had thrown themselves under it for protection.

Ben Hur was another memorable film. As I watched Ben Hur racing the obnoxious Messala in his chariot I bobbed up and down in my seat, gripped by excitement, yelling out, "The white horses, the white horses!"

Everybody was standing up, shouting encouragement, warning Ben Hur about his treacherously loosened wheel, booing his adversary. Even my parents were carried away by the realism of the screen. Never had a race been more exciting, never was a victory more unanimously acclaimed with shouts, hurrahs, and the laughter of relief.

5

Finding Out

KINDERGARTEN HAD BEEN TRANSLATED into Hebrew as "Garden of Children," and since I did not know anybody who had been to one I imagined, on my first day, that any minute we would be taken to the back yard, sunk into little ditches up to our knees, and there left to grow and flower. When nothing like this happened I felt cheated.

The kindergarten mistress was known as Bat Nesher, Daughter of the Eagle. Before her arrival in Palestine from her native Russia Bat Nesher must have been called by a non-Hebrew name, but it could not have been as appropriate as Daughter of the Eagle. There was something wild and unfettered about her; you could not look at her tanned, weather-beaten face, her short-cropped mop of gray hair, and her fierce blue eyes without hearing the wind whistle over the mountain. She blended naturally with the sea, the sand, and the dilapidated little house where she ran her kindergarten, the first at Bat Galim and one of the earliest in urban Palestine.

I cannot recall any toys, and only one picture book which was too tattered to handle and too complicated to follow. There was an incomplete set of colored bricks and some glass marbles which to us were the height of sophistication. In Haifa they were called *baloras*, from I know not what language; in Tel Aviv they were *bandoras*, probably another distortion of the same source. We arrived at about 8 A.M., had a mid-morning break for whatever snack we had brought in the regulation shoulder bag, and were dismissed at midday. We sat in a circle on the stone-tiled floor—no rug, not even a rush mat—and played games, or sang, or listened to a story. Sometimes there were only five or six of us; sometimes our number swelled to a full dozen.

Three of us, all girls, used to walk home together. For some reason we had decided one day not to walk along the beach, where it would have been pleasantly cool, but across an inland stretch of wilderness fully exposed to the ruthless midday sun. The sand was scorching hot and since none of us was wearing sandals—I believe sandals were considered an unnecessary expense in summer—it felt like fire under our bare feet.

I was slowly waddling ahead, followed by Debora, who was followed by Judith, who was hitting Debora hard on her back and bottom. Debora howled pitifully while Judith went on hitting and prodding. I was too conscious of my burning feet to think of turning to see what was going on, Debora was too stupefied to attempt to run away, and Judith just went on bashing until the howls became pitiful shrieks. The bashing stopped only when Judith veered to go to her house. A moment later I turned off towards my own house, and Debora was left alone to continue her trek through the burning sands towards her parents' hut, still sobbing, but more gently now that her tormentor had let go of her.

Debora was a timid child with watery blue eyes and flaxen hair, nearly always turned out in fussy frocks which looked both formal and tatty next to the serviceable muck-around shifts other Bat Galim little girls used to wear. Her father drove a bus, and I knew that he had come from Russia; but while other Bat Galim residents who had come from Russia were known by such names as Sasha or Misha, he had to have a qualifying noun to his name. He was not just Ivan; he was Ivan the Proselyte and his little daughter was not just Debora but Debora-the-Daughter-of-the-Proselyte-Family.

Ivan's history must have been similar to that of many of his fellow proselytes. Nineteenth-century Russia had produced a number of religious sects that accepted some of the basic tenets of Judaism and were sometimes persecuted by the Czarist authorities. Some of those Judaisers, as they were called, finally embraced Judaism proper and, having broken the last barrier, took the next logical step and went to live in the Holy Land. The first batch reached the village of Hadera as early as 1895; later arrivals were directed to the villages of the Galilee. The proselytes were a hard-working lot anxious to strike roots, but they soon discovered that their orthodoxy did not impress the secular-minded Jewish settlers, while their eagerness to accept any available job for a pittance gave rise to resentment and fear. Still they persevered, learning to speak Hebrew and giving their young such biblical names as Aminadav or Gad for boys, Yael or Debora for girls.

Hitting Debora in the midday sun was a daily ritual. Judith worked silently and efficiently, I watched ill-at-ease without intervening, and Debora suffered without offering resistance. Years later I came across a Talmudic dictum comparing proselytes to an ugly skin disease, and comprehension flashed like lightning. Surely Judith had been no ordinary bully; she had been reflecting the traditionally hostile Jewish attitude to proselytes.

I saw more of Debora than most because her father's hut by the rocks was close to our house and she sometimes ventured to come out to play. We were sitting on top of Mr. Holmes's garden wall, the tallest at Bat Galim, when she whispered urgently, "You mustn't do that."

"Mustn't do what?"

"Dangle your feet."

"Oh, that," I laughed with relief. "The Holmses won't mind."

"It's not the Holmses," Debora persisted. "Dangling your feet brings bad luck."

"What will it do to me?"

"If you go on, your mother will die."

A wave of mad rage welled up in me, the sort of rage that still makes me feel murderous and impotent at the same time.

"You're lying!" I screamed. "You're lying!"

I defiantly dangled my feet several more times, my heart pounding with rage and fear, then jumped down from the tall wall—something I would never dare do again—and ran back home to find my mother peacefully shelling peas.

"Debora is no liar," mother said. "She's superstitious."

It was difficult to understand what superstition was. I explained it to myself as something which Bat Galim children would be better off without, and which the children of Ivan the Proselyte had plenty of, on account of their parents having brought it with them from Russia.

One hot afternoon I was made to comb my hair and was taken by bus to the Old City to see a traveling circus from Egypt. I saw a huge gray animal with a trunk and tusks, and was told it was an elephant. It did not seem real. The real animals were those I could see at Bat Galim, donkeys, mules, horses, and camels. Donkeys with bells tied to their necks came to the seafront every morning to be loaded with sand which was later sold to building contractors for mixing with cement. The quarrying of sand at Bat Galim was prohibited by law, but the donkeymen were never caught and the gentle tide discreetly smoothed away the gaping cavities left by the daily pillage.

Sometimes I saw a caravan of sand-colored camels trotting along the seafront, led by a rider on a black donkey.

"The donkey goes first to set a measured pace," I was told. "Without him the camels would run like mad."

The camels were aloof and graceful, retreating into the

distance and blending with the sand. They were on their way towards a sand dune called desert, which was a place with no sea, no shade, and no drinking water. They fed off their humps and when their riders were about to die of thirst they galloped unerringly towards a place called oasis, where there was sure to be a spring of fresh water and a clump of date palms.

One summer evening lots of people were sitting cross-legged on the floor of the kitchen veranda and singing "The Song of the Caravan." A voice began:

The desert
Will carry us
On camels' humps.

The rest of us sang the refrain like an incantation:

Carry us, O Desert,
Carry us
On camels' humps.

The song, anonymously composed in one of the kibbutzim, was one of those early attempts to fuse European and Oriental musical elements. There was the sentimental tune, the trill associated with the Arab shepherd's reed-pipe, the exciting syncopation, the sound of camel bells, and the lingering echo. It was a haunting tune, clutching at the heart and evoking the mystery of the desert.

The occasion must have been a farewell party for some of my father's brothers who had despaired of ever eking out a living from the small Metulla homestead and were about to emigrate. Those were the years of unemployment and despondency. Jewish farmers had little use for Jewish field hands and preferred cheap Arab labor. Young pioneers as well as older residents counted themselves lucky if they secured a few days' work chopping stones for government-sponsored road works side by side with seasoned Arab workers. Some members of the recently formed

Regiment of Labor returned in desperation to their native Russia to join a Soviet project for Jewish agricultural settlements in the Crimea. In 1923 more than three thousand left Palestine out of a total Jewish population of 90,000. Between 1926 and 1928 many more thousands emigrated, among them three of my Metulla uncles, who had decided to try their luck in such exotic-sounding countries as Colombia, Brazil, and Cuba.

On the night of the party I noticed that many of the guests were smoking cigarettes. There was no oil lamp on the veranda and the cigarettes gleamed in the dark like the stars above our heads. It was beautiful.

"Why don't you smoke?" I said reproachfully to my father when the uncles had departed.

"I hate smoking," he answered angrily. "It pollutes the air. We live in an unspoiled country. Let's keep it that way."

Next thing I knew we had a pipe-smoking uncle about the house. He was my mother's brother from Warsaw who had recently settled in Tel Aviv and came to visit us with his wife and youngest daughter Hanna. Hanna had one blue eye and one brown one, and we had a marvelous time on the seafront.

Mother had told me that her brother was called Nahum, but when I addressed him by that name he looked surprised.

"Aren't you going to call me *Uncle* Nahum?"

"Nahum is nicer."

"Why?"

"Because you have ginger hair, and you wear glasses, and you smoke a pipe, and anyhow Uncle is silly."

For a moment he was dumbfounded, then he burst into uproarious laughter. "Mania," he called to my mother. "You've got a real little savage here."

Uncle Nahum, who as Dr. Nir became in 1959 the Speaker of the Israel Knesset, was a few years younger than my mother. They had been very close during their Warsaw days, but while mother settled in Palestine as early as 1908, he stayed behind for seventeen more years, studying and then practicing law in St. Petersburg and Warsaw. On his arrival in Palestine in 1925 he started a practice in Tel Aviv while his wife, a dentist, followed her own profession. They had taken a rambling apartment in Ahad Haam Street where one room served as a lawyer's office, another as a dentist's surgery and the rest, two or three pokey little holes, as living quarters for themselves and their two daughters. The office had a leather-upholstered settee with armchairs to match, and smelled of tobacco. The surgery had various instruments of torture on display, including a drill which looked like a crossbow and which my aunt worked with a treadle. When we were visiting I slept in the surgery while my mother was put up on the office settee.

Uncle Nahum was a leading member of *Poaley Zion Smol*, the left wing of the Workers of Zion party. Whenever we were visiting he was holding meetings in his office and addressing them in a guttural language which I did not understand but which I had learned to call jargon. It was quite distinct from the sing-song Polish he spoke with his wife and daughters.

"Why do you speak jargon?" I asked him after one of his meetings. With me he spoke Hebrew.

"Jargon is not a name of a language," he corrected me. "The language you heard me speak is called Yiddish."

"Why do you speak Yiddish then?" I persisted. "It's so ugly."

"That's an arrogant, ignorant thing to say. Yiddish is the language of the Jews. We in Palestine should speak Yiddish as well as Hebrew."

Uncle Nahum was advocating the official *Poaley Zion* policy which claimed Yiddish as the rallying language of world Jewry. In Palestine, however, the cause of Yiddish was not popular; a new generation was growing up which took pride in reviving the Hebrew of the Bible and looked down upon Yiddish, derived from medieval Low German, as a relic of ghetto mentality. At four or five I did not understand the thinking behind this attitude, but I already accepted the view that Yiddish was jargon, spoken by people too old to learn Hebrew, too tied up with an inglorious past.

My ignorance of Yiddish accounted for the lack of communication between myself and my mother's mother on the only occasion she came to stay with us at Bat Galim. My Warsaw grandparents had followed in their daughter's footsteps and settled in Palestine well before the First World War. Old Mr. Raphelkes had always been a Zionist. Even before my mother was born he had joined a Warsaw Zionist Society called *Menuha Ve Nahala*, Rest and Patrimony, which in 1890 went on to found the village of Rehovot. After my mother had settled down in Haifa, he sold his boot factory and retired to Rehovot, living in his own bungalow and employing hired labor to look after his almond orchard.

Mr. Raphelkes never visited his daughter in Haifa. He had forgiven her youthful rebellion over her university education, but he could not bring himself to forgive her choice of husband. He had no use for a son-in-law who never went to synagogue, never prayed, never observed any of the dietary laws, and spent the Holy Sabbath traipsing round the countryside in hobnailed boots like a gentile. He vowed he would never set foot in such an un-Jewish household. His only concession was to allow mother to visit him at Rehovot, so that he could enjoy his grandchildren. I never knew him. He died the day I was born and was buried in Jerusalem on the Mount of Olives. His widow, after her one visit to Bat Galim, died too and was buried at Rehovot. For many years afterwards a sack of almonds would mysteriously arrive each autumn at Bat

Galim and mother would ruefully say, "It's from Rehovot. That's all my father left me."

The almond orchard had passed into the hands of Aunt Helena, mother's eldest sister, who had also settled at Rehovot with her husband. Traveling from Bat Galim to visit them at Rehovot, about fourteen miles south of Tel Aviv, was a complicated undertaking. First we caught the local Arab bus to Carmel Railway Station, where the train was meant to make the occasional scheduled stop, but since nobody knew the schedule, it was safer to start waving at the Arab engine driver the moment the train came into view. We changed at Lydda Junction and after a long delay reached Tel Aviv Station where we clambered onto a bus run by a Jewish cooperative serving South Judea. The last hundred yards or so had to be walked along a path made of sand and clots of red soil. It was a full day's journey.

I was taken to a small cemetery to see a grave with a eucalyptus tree growing over it.

"This is your grandmother's grave," mother said.

I wished myself back on the seafront of Bat Galim. I missed the thud of the waves lulling me to sleep and I did not like Aunt Helena's cooking. She ruined the lovely crisp carrots by stewing them with sugar and mashing them into a mess called *tzimmes* and was surprised when I pulled a face at beetroot soup called *borsch*, dumplings called *knoedlach*, stuffed dough bags called *kreplach*, and dough ribbons called *lokshen*.

"What do you eat then?" Aunt Helena wondered.

"Why, eggplant," I answered, astonished at such ignorance.

My mother was a wizard with eggplants, having learned the art of cooking them from the Arab peasant women who came to help with the weekly wash and the housework. She peeled them, cut them into flat round slices, and put them out in the sun to bake away their initial bitterness.

Then she fried them and served them on slices of bread. Sometimes she grilled a large eggplant whole until it was slightly charred, spooned out the inside without the bitter seeds, mashed it with a hard-boiled egg, dressed it with lemon juice, olive oil, salt and garlic, garnished it with sliced tomatoes, and served it as a cold dish. At the beginning of summer, when eggplants were small and hard, she pickled them in large glass jars, having first sent us children scurrying in the fields to pick up some dill. A washerwoman had told us that no Arab maiden was worth her bride price until she was able to cook eggplants in seven different ways. Mother learned all seven, and I intended to do the same when I grew up.

6

Hadar Hacarmel

NOBODY HAD WARNED ME that we were going to leave our lovely house by the sea and move into a rented apartment at Hadar Hacarmel, a dignified-looking suburb on the lower slopes of Mount Carmel. I did not realize that we were about to move until a mule-drawn wagon pulled up by the side gate and removal men started loading it with furniture. It was a long drive to the new place. When we arrived I saw my first three-story house.

Hadar Hacarmel, the Glory of Mount Carmel, came into being about 1905, when Haifa became an important link on the newly constructed Hejaz Railway, but its real expansion began only in the mid-twenties. Its houses were made of white stone and were easily distinguishable by their picturesque balconies, ornamental columns, oddly shaped windows, and gables. Some were family houses; others had been designed as apartment houses, spacious enough to accommodate three or four families each. Many had flowers, cypresses, and olive trees growing around them.

The system of numbering houses had not yet reached Palestine and the only way to identify a house was by the name of its owner. We lived in Shapira's House in Nordau Street; a family we knew lived in Tchlenoff's House in Herzl Street; a girl I was to become friendly with lived in Rachkowsky's House in Pevsner Street. If you did not know where a particular house was located, there was no logical way of looking for it. Inquiries from passersby adhered to a standard opening formula:

"Excuse me, where is Zimmerman's House around here?"

"Excuse me, where is Mizrahi's House around here?"

"Excuse me, where is Reinin's House around here?"

The answers varied, but on the whole they too ran to a pattern:

"Zimmerman's House around here?"

"That's right, Zimmerman's House in Nordau Street."

"This is Nordau Street all right. But Zimmerman's House? Wait a minute, isn't it that big house immediately past Steiner's House?"

"I don't know Steiner's House."

"You don't know Steiner's House? Everybody knows Steiner's House. Hey, Arie," the helpful local would call to a friend spotted on the other side of the street. "Come over here for a moment. Isn't Steiner's House the one with the trees?"

"Steiner has had the trees cut down," Arie would say importantly. "He's extending the property and putting up a third story."

"Steiner is putting up a third story? That's interesting. Tell me, who's the contractor?"

"Rubinstein. Good chap Rubinstein is. Uses only Hebrew labor."

"He would be in trouble if he didn't. We won't stand for Arab labor here."

While the conversation digressed, the forgotten questor would ask again, this time less politely: "Where's Zimmerman's House? I'm asking you."

"We've already told you. Didn't you hear? It's the big one past Steiner's House, which is the one with a heap of sand and cement where the trees used to be."

Our own apartment, at Shapira's House, was part of a large three-story stone building, with flower beds and gravel paths in front and an uncultivated patch of soil at the back. During the summer months a gardener came every evening to water the flowers. Water at Hadar Hacarmel came out of taps fed by the municipal water supply. The garden tap was the responsibility of the landlord, and the gardener had instructions to lock it after use to stop us children squirting water on each other and wasting what in a sun-scorched country was a precious commodity.

We lived on the ground floor, in a peculiarly designed apartment where each room followed the next like a chain of dominoes, most of them opening onto a large semicircular veranda; after we moved out, it was converted into a café. Like all Hadar Hacarmel dwelling houses it had electricity, which for a Bat Galim child was a novelty. I tried all the switches one by one and then turned my attention to the wall sockets. I had been told that if you plugged in the two pins at the end of the desk lamp cord, a light would come on. I wanted to find out what would happen if I plugged in two of my mother's discarded hatpins. Nothing happened. Most of the sockets were dead, either because of incorrect wiring or poor workmanship.

We no longer had any pets and my attempts to bring home stray kittens and puppies were firmly discouraged. I was allowed, however, to play in the street. After the roadlessness of Bat Galim's sand dunes, the gravel-made streets of Hadar Hacarmel felt wonderfully solid under my feet in spite of their rough uneven surface. There was hardly any traffic and what little there was ran mostly through Herzl Street and spiral Burgh Road leading to the Old City. Steep Balfour Street, today one of Hadar Hacarmel's main thoroughfares, was an ideal place to muck around after the occasional rainfall, when streams of water rushed down the mountain slopes and turned it into a river. While adults dropped in stones to step across on, we children rearranged them to create dams and waterfalls.

My own road, Nordau Street, was fairly flat and therefore an obvious running track despite its many bumps and pitfalls. Several times a day we had to interrupt a race to make way for a swiftly moving line of donkeys carrying sand to building sites in the neighborhood.

"*Hawalak! Hawalak!* Gee up, gee up!" the Arab donkeymen shouted. I wondered if the black donkeys, with bells and beads hung around their necks, were my old pals from the seafront.

Sometimes I played with a girl called Malka whose parents, immigrants from England, lived on the floor above us. Malka was a pretty child, with dark hair and a peach complexion, gentle and well-mannered, while I was still a Bat Galim barbarian who preferred to run around barefoot. Mother was very conscious of my barbarism and decreed that, whatever leeway I was given in the mornings, in the afternoons I would get "dressed" like all the other good little girls of our Hadar Hacarmel set. Every afternoon, when the sun was still unbearably hot and the air without a trace of cooling breeze, I was made to put on a well-ironed frock, knee-high white stocking, and white canvas shoes.

"Now you can go upstairs to see Malka."

I had not been long at Hadar Hacarmel when Malka took me behind the house and showed me a booth which her father had built. It was made of rush mats fastened to wooden frames and hung with palm fronds, red apples, and colored paper flags. She said it was a *sukka* and explained that her family would be taking their meals in it throughout the eight days of *Sukkot,* the Feast of Tabernacles.

I marveled. My father's idea of celebrating the Feast of Tabernacles, or any other religious holiday for that matter, was to organize a hike to an unexplored part of the country, while mother held, like some of the Talmud sages nineteen centuries earlier, that living in the Land of Israel and taking part in its rebuilding was as pleasing to God as any act of worship. The result was that I grew up a total stranger to religious practice. When Malka reported my ignorance to her father, he offered to improve matters by taking me to synagogue on *Simhat Tora,* a celebration marking the completion of the annual cycle of the Pentateuch synagogue reading and the commencement of a repeat cycle.

On the day, Malka and I were dressed like twin sisters in white frocks, white stockings, and white shoes, given a colored flag each with an apple impaled on its pole, and led a long way from home. My first glimpse of the Hadar Hacarmel synagogue revealed a low oblong building, made of unpainted concrete, bare of trees and shrubbery. Malka took me up a flight of stairs to the women's gallery, which commanded an excellent view of the hall below, where the men were beginning to assemble. Nothing much seemed to be happening until some people took the Scrolls of the Law out of the Ark and started walking around with them. The scrolls looked beautiful in their velvet wraps richly embroidered with gold and silver. Malka said we were supposed to kiss them, so we went downstairs into the main hall and mingled with the jubilant crowd of men, pushing and shoving with the best of them. The scroll carries were doing the *hakafot,* the rounds, each walking with his precious burden seven times around the hall. Malka and I exerted ourselves to kiss each scroll as many times as possible on each of its seven rounds and tried to beat each other's record.

My only other religious experience had taken place when we were still living at Bat Galim. Some half a dozen men in long black coats and black hats were standing on the dry rocky surface of the seabed opposite our house. The sea was out and the men seemed to be following it.

"Mum," I said anxiously, "they're going in with their clothes on."

"No dear, they're not. See, they've stopped. They are praying."

"Why are they praying by the sea?"

"It's the eve of the Day of Atonement. They are performing the *tashlich*. They are asking God to forgive them their misdeeds and are casting them into the sea."

I felt confident that my lovely Bat Galim sea could cleanse any sins cast into it and was wondering whether I could cast some of my own when mother continued: "On the Day of Atonement God forgives only sins committed against himself. He cannot forgive you sins you have committed against fellow creatures. For those you have to call on the person you have sinned against and ask him to forgive you."

"Can we ask forgiveness only on the Day of Atonement?"

Mother laughed. "It's possible to ask forgiveness any time, but particularly on the Day of Atonement."

"And if your friend doesn't want to forgive you?"

"You've got to go on asking. Once upon a time a great sage offended a friend of his. On the Day of Atonement the sage went to his friend and asked to be forgiven. 'I won't forgive you,' the friend said. The following year the sage went around again to ask forgiveness. 'I won't forgive you,' the friend said. This happened nine times. Only on the tenth Day of Atonement did the friend forgive the great sage and the sin was cleansed."

"Ten years?" I was incredulous. A year seemed a very long time to wait for forgiveness, and ten years were altogether beyond my grasp. The whole thing belonged to a world which had little to do with reality.

Reality was all around me, and it was full of revelations. First there was that derelict back garden, with large boulders which begged to be rolled along. Once I lifted one to discover a black scorpion underneath; on another occasion I discovered a yellow one and my brother said it was even deadlier than the black kind. He also told me that if you poured methylated spirit around a scorpion and lit it, the scorpion would sting itself to death; my father, however, said that a scorpion committing suicide was not a scientific fact but merely folklore.

There was also our mysterious landlord who lived with his family on the top floor. Whenever I passed by I saw him messing around in a large basement room at the back of the house. It had been designed as a communal laundry room with sinks, taps, and shelves, but Mr. Shapira had requisitioned it for his own use. When I peeped through the windows to see what he was up to, I saw a pile of oranges on the floor, primus stoves, test tubes, and glass jars of all shapes and sizes.

"He's turned it into a laboratory," mother said. "He's experimenting."

A faint memory stirred in my mind.

"With beer?"

"What an extraordinary idea. Mr. Shapira is a research chemist. He's trying to make orange concentrate. When oranges are out of season we'll mix it with water and have lovely orange juice all the year round."

There was a strong smell of decaying orange peel and burnt sugar, which I was taught to call caramel. As time went by I got used to it and just kept prowling around the basement in the hope of being offered some of the experimental concentrate. Mr. Shapira, bent over his test tubes in a white overall, never noticed me. In due course he transferred his experiments to Tel Aviv and jointly founded the firm of *Assiss,* meaning juice, which has since become known in many parts of the world for its fruit juices and preserves.

7

The Battle of the Languages

SHORTLY AFTER WE MOVED to Hadar Hacarmel mother took
me to see the Hebrew Reali School, where I would attend
Form One at the beginning of the new term. She was
showing me how to find my way back home through the
walled forecourt of the nearby Technion when I noticed an
old man slowly walking ahead of us. Halfway across the
forecourt he stopped in front of the magnificent Technion
building and surveyed it for a moment. Then he began
climbing the wide marble steps.

"That's Mr. Baerwald," my mother whispered rever-
ently. "He's the man who built the Technion and your
school."

Alexander Baerwald, one of Palestine's first Jewish ar-
chitects, was about fifty when I caught a glimpse of him,
but by childish definition he was old, for he went about
dressed in a city suit and moved slowly. The banisters on
either side of the wide front steps of the Technion were
made of smooth slabs of stone. By the time Mr. Baerwald
had reached the top step and stopped for breath, I had run
up and glided down them twice.

The Hebrew Technion, Israel's Institute of Technical En-
gineering, has since moved most of its departments to a
new campus on the slopes of Mount Carmel, but the
original building is still one of Haifa's proud landmarks.
To me it looked like a palace, with its yellow sandstone
walls, its wide marble front steps, its arches, rows of win-

dows and quasi-battlements. The grounds were beautifully landscaped, sloping gently into another plateau where the Hebrew Reali School came into view. It was another palace, made of the same yellow sandstone, with open corridors not unlike cloisters, battlements, and a small turret. The two buildings were the most beautiful I had ever seen.

While admiring their beauty, I wondered why my school went by the name of the *Hebrew* Reali School, when there was no non-Hebrew Reali school to confuse it with, and why the Technion was called the *Hebrew* Technion when it was the only one in Palestine. The emphasis on "Hebrew" seemed unnecessary and somewhat funny. I had been a schoolgirl for several years before I learned that this was a relic from what came to be known in the history of modern Jewish Palestine as the Battle of the Languages.

It had started with well-intentioned philanthropy. In 1901 a group of German Jews launched a relief organization to improve the social and political conditions of their brethren in Eastern Europe and the Orient. Education was considered a priority and the *Hilfsverein der deutschen Juden* opened schools for Jewish children in many backward countries, with German as the main language of instruction. In Palestine those schools were popularly known as Ezra Schools, *ezra* being the Hebrew for *Hilf*, help.

Soon the *Hilfsverein* conceived the ambitious idea of establishing in Palestine an Institute of Technology as well as a secondary school to produce acceptable students for it. A vast plot was acquired for the purpose in Haifa, and the design of the two buildings was entrusted to Alexander Baerwald, a young Jewish architect who had already made a name for himself in his native Germany. Although German-trained and not a resident of Palestine, Baerwald decided not to impose alien western conceptions on an eastern landscape and tried to evolve an original Jewish style emulating ancient Muslim architecture.

He started with the *Technikum*, to use the institute's original German name. The cornerstone was laid in 1912 and the following year the first classes were held. Then all hell broke loose.

The *Hilfsverein* board of governors had decided that the language of instruction at the *Technikum* would be German, as it was at all its other schools. The decision had been passed by a majority vote, overruling a minority plea that no cultural revival could come about in Eretz Israel in any language but Hebrew. When the first classes were conducted in German, the National Association of Teachers, formed ten years earlier, called on members to ban teaching at the Technion and asked would-be students not to enroll. Other *Hilfsverein* schools all over the country struck in sympathy. An impasse was reached; the *Hilfsverein* would not reverse its original decision, the Teachers' Association would not allow any teaching at the Technion in any language other than Hebrew. The magnificent building remained unused. When a year later war broke out, the Turks converted it into a military hospital and when they were driven out, the British used it for their own sick and wounded. The turning point came well after the war, when the World Zionist Organization acquired the property from the *Hilfsverein* and pronounced in favor of Hebrew. The first regular classes at university level began towards the end of 1924, and the following year Alexander Baerwald became the first head of the institute's department of architecture.

The beginnings of the nearby Reali School were equally stormy. When the *Hilfsverein* first made known its plan to build it, there was great jubilation. But in 1913, when the board of governors decreed that the language of instruction would be German, the mood changed.

There was no need to call a teachers' strike, as in the case of the Technion, since the project was still on the drawing board. But a group of Haifa teachers, who were to form the nucleus of the academic staff, decided to oppose the resolution anyhow. The headmaster-designate, whom the Haifa nucleus had not met, was Dr. Arthur Biram, a distinguished biblical scholar who was still teaching in Berlin. While preparing to leave for Haifa Dr. Biram met my father, who was completing his biology course at the University of Berlin, and invited him to join the staff of the new school. Father and mother and their first-born daughter were living at a boarding house run by a well-known Zionist family.

"We shall have to teach the boys Talmud," Dr. Biram told his prospective recruit.

"What about the girls?"

"I visualize it as a boys' school."

My father was taken aback. The tendency in secular circles in Palestine was to establish co-educational schools. The Herzlia Gymnasium in Tel Aviv was co-educational; the primitive Avtalia, precursor of the proposed Reali School, had been co-educational. Father tried to avoid the issue.

"My subject is biology."

"The Talmud is an essential part of a decent Jewish education," Dr. Biram stated, eyeing my father suspiciously.

"Hebrew is an essential part of a decent Jewish education," father corrected, trying to bring up the burning issue of the moment.

The two men parted unsure of each other. A couple of months later news reached my father in Berlin that Dr. Biram had defied the *Hilfsverein* and started the projected Reali School on his own in a rented Arab house. On his return to Haifa father joined Dr. Biram's staff as master of biology. There were about sixty children at school, all boys, but when war broke out girls were admitted too. The school has remained co-educational ever since.

The war years brought call-up orders for some of the

staff. Father hid in a Druze village where the conscripting officer did not dare follow him, but Dr. Biram was caught. Generations of Reali schoolchildren gleefully repeated the story, apocryphal no doubt, of how he had jumped into an empty sauerkraut barrel hoping to remain undetected and how, being too corpulent to squeeze himself fully in, he was hauled out and brought before the conscripting officer. School lore also had it that Dr. Biram gravely informed the officer that since he had been born on February 29 and was able to mark his birthday only once in four years, he was not thirty-six but only nine, and therefore under military age. He was sent to the wars all the same but as a German subject fared somewhat better than the Ottoman conscripts.

After the war, when the World Zionist Organization acquired the Technion from the unrepentant *Hilfsverein*, Alexander Baerwald was allowed to proceed with the original plan for the Reali School, and in 1922 it was completed in all its glory. Dr. Biram had in the meantime returned safely to his post and in due course turned the school into one of Palestine's foremost institutions of education. To drive home the point over which the Battle of the Languages had been fought, it was officially named the *Hebrew* Reali School, and the Technion was likewise named the *Hebrew* Technion. The *Hilfsverein* was dissolved in 1939.

8

School

MY FIRST DAY at the Hebrew Reali School was inauspicious.
I had arrived late and was ushered into a room where
about a dozen boys and girls were already seated behind
small desks. They had sheets of paper in front of them and
were busily drawing with colored pencils. The teacher
was a robust woman with black hair and a stern face. She
pointed to the colored drawings pinned to the walls and
to the painted cardboard elephant, cows, and trees displayed on a shelf, and said with pride, "You see these
lovely things? They were done by last year's pupils. Now
you can make some too."

I knew immediately that I would never make cardboard
elephants, cows, and trees and I did not much want to
either, because I did not think they were at all lovely. A
few weeks later, when it was reported that I had made no
progress in making cardboard figures, my mother got up
from her siesta somewhat earlier than usual and said,
"Let's play a game."

She made me sit next to her at the breakfast table and
emptied out a boxful of small white cards with black lines
drawn on them. The lines looked like matchsticks, some
lying across one another, some arranged into funny
shapes. I thought one looked like a tent and another like
my comb, which had only few teeth left. Mother arranged three cards in a row and pushed them in front of
me.

"This says *Mum*," she said.

She arranged three more cards. "And that says *Dad*."

It looked like fun. "Now make them say *donkey*," I asked.

She arranged some cards to say donkey and promised that if I could remember how to arrange them for myself she would show me some more tricks the following afternoon. We kept playing until one afternoon mother informed me that I could read and that the school had agreed to move me up to a higher form.

At that time a child's first school year was mostly spent on handicraft and storytelling; the business of reading and writing was seriously tackled only in the second year. My mother's feat of teaching a child to read in three or four weeks and, furthermore, of prevailing upon the school authorities to let a beginner join the older age group in Form Two, was a nine-day wonder. Neighbors came to congratulate her and Mrs. Shapira, the wife of the orange juice experimenter, presented us with a plateful of kohlrabi, a variety of cabbage with a turnip-shaped stem, which one ate raw.

There was indeed cause for congratulations. Education in mandatory Palestine, unlike present-day Israel, had to be paid for all the way through. Reducing my projected term of schooling by one year, with no damage done to academic standards, was a great saving in a family with three children. The timing was particularly propitious because my father had taken a year's leave of absence to follow a further course of study in Berlin, and money was short. He wrote to congratulate me and we took to sending each other little notes, I in my large round scrawl, he in his tiny but legible scholar's hand. He wrote that Berlin was covered in snow and he was putting some in the envelope for me to see. I already knew that snow, like hail, was something which melted quickly, but I peered hopefully into the empty envelope all the same.

The port of Jaffa circa 1908
(Courtesy Jewish National Fund Picture Collection)

With my mother, who
taught Hebrew to
immigrants until her
death at the age of 87

My father, founder of the
Haifa Institute of Biology
which was later named
Bet Pinhas after him

In the sea of Bat Galim, my sister *(far right)* and brother *(second from left)* and the Holmes children

The Hebrew Technion in 1934, with a bare Mount Carmel in the background *(Courtesy Jewish National Fund Picture Collection)*

The Chimney Waterfall at Metulla *(Courtesy Jewish National Fund Picture Collection)*

Schoolchildren's procession during the 1934 Festival
of the First Fruits
(Courtesy Jewish National Fund Picture Collection)

The Hebrew Reali School in 1926
(Courtesy Jewish National Fund Picture Collection)

My sister Yardena in her
own choreography as the
Witch of En Dor

My father with my
brother Gideon, who later
was Agricultural
Councillor at the Israel
Embassy in Washington

Bo-Kah

My teacher in Form Two was a plump, pale-faced young woman who instructed us to address her by her biblical first name of Pua preceded by *gveret,* a title which means both Miss and Mrs., and Pua she remained to generations of pupils even when she had obtained her Ph.D. in Berlin and become known in educational circles as Dr. P. Menczel. When we met in London after an interval of nearly forty years she was still as I remembered her, plump, vivacious, and dedicated, only her silky black hair had turned gray.

Whatever she taught, she put her heart into: writing, sums, singing, good manners, and cleanliness. There was a little boy called Dodi who had been warned time and again not to turn up in class unwashed. When warnings remained unheeded, Miss Pua picked him up, lowered him into the classroom sink, and washed his dirty feet and legs with her own hands.

When it was too hot to stay indoors Miss Pua gave us our lessons under the shady locust-bean tree in the school garden. She took us for walks on the Technion grounds and pointed out the various plants. The pink, clock-faced flowers with fleshy finger-shaped leaves were called Noon Flowers, because they opened at noon and closed at sunset. There were carnations and roses, sunflowers and hollyhocks; and there was a tree with deceptively attractive fruit which we were taught to call Sodom apples, because they were poisonous. Miss Pua pointed to a coniferous shrub.

"This one is called thuya. It's also called the Tree of Life, because it's green all the year round. In Latin it's called *arbor vitae.*"

"What's Latin?" I piped, but I was not heard.

"What's Latin?" I asked when I got home.

"It's a dead language," mother said.

"What's a dead language?"

"People don't speak it any more; they only learn how to read it."

"Can you read it?"

"Well, I was taught to when I was at the Russian gymnasium."

"Will I be taught to read it?"

"Not in this country you won't," mother chuckled, and I did not know whether I ought to feel relieved or deprived.

An essential part of the school curriculum was Knowledge of the Country, and from time to time we were driven in a hired bus to places of interest. One such place was the village of Nahalal, founded in 1921, the first smallholders' cooperative settlement in the valley of Jezreel. It had been built in a circle, and to demonstrate this unique feature the driver drove us around and around until a girl at the back became sick. We were shown a cow shed, a granary, and the latest agricultural innovation, a plow without oxen called a tractor.

On another occasion we were taken to see the new Shemen soap factory in the bay of Acre. We looked down into a well full of thick yellow liquid and were told that it would eventually become *sabon*. I did not understand.

"It's simple," Dodi tried to explain. "When the stuff hardens they cut it up into cakes and that's *sabon*."

"What do you do with it?"

Dodi was embarrassed. "Er . . . you wash your hands and feet with it."

"Oh," the light dawned. "You mean that's how they make *borit*?"

"*Borit*? What a funny word."

I later learned that *sabon*, the popular word for soap, had been derived from the French *savon*, whereas *borit*, the word used at home by my purist parents, was biblical. I clung to my *borit* for several years but eventually gave up, recognizing that *sabon* had become as undisputably Hebrew as *otoboos* for autobus.

On our return from the Shemen factory we were made to write a brief account of the day. Miss Pua made us write as often as possible and gave us regular homework. One assignment was to write a self-portrait and state a professional ambition.

"When I grow up," I wrote, "I am going to be a piano teacher."

It was the most glamorous profession I could think of. Other girls wrote that they would like to be doctors, or dressmakers, or nurses. Not one little girl ever doubted that she would go out to work when she grew up, and not one little boy ever thought otherwise. Most of us had the example of our parents before us. Aviva's mother was a midwife; Meir's mother was a doctor; and Penina's mother cooked and served lunches in her house for regular patrons.

Work, however, belonged to the distant future; the present was for learning. There was a black cupboard in the classroom which Miss Pua called the library. My first library book was a story about a baby who had been too tightly swathed. After that I was given the Hebrew translations of *Alice in Wonderland,* the *Adventures of Baron Munchausen,* and Charles and Mary Lamb's *Tales from Shakespeare.* When I had exhausted the black cupboard I was sent to a lending library in Herzl Street which was the sideline of the local stationer. It had several shelves stacked with books in Russian and German, which my mother used to borrow, and a section for children's books in Hebrew. For two piasters a month I was allowed to change books six times a week. Reading became an addiction.

Most children's books were translations from foreign

- 79 -

languages. I had no guidance other than my own random choice and, sometimes, other children's recommendations.

"Have you read *White Fang*?" Meir asked as he bumped into me in the library. "You must read it, it's lovely." He pronounced it *White Pang*, since in Hebrew no word can start with an *F*.

"Who is it by?" I asked. I had just been taught that for some odd reason books had to be identified not only by their titles but also by the names of their authors.

"Gak London," Meir said, pleased at being able to supply the information. His mispronunciation was due to the fact that Hebrew has no such native sound as *J* as in Jack or G as in George. Translators faced with the task of transcribing the sound had to invent a sign for it. Some added an apostrophe to the Hebrew symbol of *Y*; others appended it to the symbol of *G*; but youngsters like us who had never been taught that a comma hanging over a letter had any particular significance just ignored it and gave the Hebrew symbols their native sound, pronouncing Jack as *Gak* or *Yak*, depending on the transcription read.

"*White Pang* by Gak London was lovely," I enthusiastically agreed the following afternoon. I recommended *Tom Sawyer* by Mark Tven, Hebrew having no such sound as *W*.

I had not been at school for more than a year when a new building had to be added to accommodate the growing number of schoolchildren in a fast-expanding town. It was to house the lower forms only, and we took a proprietary interest in its progress. We watched the builders dig the foundations and waited eagerly for the moment when they would put a small charge of dynamite under an undiggable rock, light the wick, and run away shouting in Arabic, "*Warda, warda barood!* Explosion on the way!"

When a *warda* warning was heard all human traffic came to a standstill until the sound of the explosion, followed by a shower of broken rock and a whiff of gunpowder, announced the all-clear. In Haifa, with its rocky soil and much building going on, such explosions were frequent and the warning as familiar as any street cry.

"Why are you late?" the gym mistress asked a girl called Yael Weizman whose little brother Ezer was tagging behind her.

"We had to stop for the *warda barood*," Yael answered and the boy, who in 1977 became Israel's Minister of Defense, nodded affirmation. The excuse was accepted. You could never be too careful. Sometimes the wick burned more slowly than anticipated and a foolhardy person venturing out prematurely was likely to be caught in a belated explosion.

In class we were busy composing a message of dedication to be preserved forever under the foundations of the new wing. When the day arrived for laying the cornerstone Meir and I were chosen to put the message in place.

We reported in the afternoon wearing white, white being the regulation color for festive occasions. At the appointed hour the rolled sheet of paper with the message of dedication was pushed into a bottle, and the bottle sealed and lowered into the ground. There were lots of speeches. One of the speakers said that if ever, hundreds of years hence, the new wing should be demolished and the bottle retrieved, the message of dedication composed by the lower forms and put in place by Meir and myself would be an historic document. We felt very important.

By that time my class had moved up a form. My new teacher was *adon* Avraham, Mr. Avraham, but we were also allowed to address him by the more familiar *mori*, My Teacher. Mr. Avraham had the gift of inspiring his pupils with a craving for knowledge. Whether he was teaching the stories of the Bible or initiating us into the complicated art of conjugating a verb, he made it feel like an adventure. Time and again the bell would catch us unawares and a frustrated chorus would call out in unison: "So soon?" Every day he opened a new door for us into the unknown; I began to be conscious of my environment, the countries outside Palestine, history.

To me Mr. Avraham seemed an adult person, for he was a teacher, but I later learned that he was only nineteen at the time. After two years' teaching he left for the States to study archaeology and, as Dr. A. Biran, was Israel's consul general in Los Angeles in the mid-fifties. In 1979 I called on him in Jerusalem, where he is now director of the Hebrew Union College. At near seventy Professor Biran was hardly any different from the young teacher I adored, his hair still light brown, his eyes still sparkling, and his charm undiminished.

I suspect Mr. Avraham did not have much of a singing voice, for one morning, after he had written on the blackboard the words of a new song, he asked Miss Pua to come in and teach it to us. The words, although written in Hebrew characters, were in a foreign tongue. Mr. Avraham said it was an African language. I then heard for the first time of the proposed Jewish State in Uganda, one of the most painful issues in the early history of Zionism.

When Dr. Theodor Herzl, father of modern Zionism, had to accept that the Turkish Sultan was not amenable to the idea of a national Jewish entity in Palestine under the Ottoman aegis, he began looking elsewhere. In 1903 he put before the Sixth Zionist Congress a British offer to establish an autonomous Jewish settlement in Uganda. The Uganda of 1903 was not the territory known today by that name; it formed part of British East Africa and is now in northeast Kenya. It was available for resettlement because recent tribal wars had left it depopulated.

A Jewish national home outside Eretz Israel ran counter to the very foundations of Zionism, but so great was the longing for autonomy and so pressing the need to find a haven for persecuted Jews that a resolution was passed by a majority of 295 against 178, with 100 abstentions, to send out a commission to investigate Uganda's suitability for Jewish settlement. The anti-Ugandists felt betrayed. As the sessions wore on, they blackened their faces like savages and leaped on their opponents in the congress corridors baring their teeth and uttering jungle war cries. My mother, who in 1903 was a student in Geneva and attended the congress in Basel as a matter of course, later told me that it was a black day for Zionism.

The following year Herzl died and the Uganda project was shelved, but not before a group of Jewish students had composed, in earnest or in jest, what was described as the national anthem of the future Jewish state in Uganda. The words were meant to be an imitation of an African dialect, mere sounds without sense. We sang them in the approximate pronunciation taught us by Mr. Avraham:

> Chin qua
> Cheni meni cheni meni
> Yassen yassen chin qua qua, chin qua qua.
> Kalekatin
> Hocher va rumba, hocher va rumba
> Hocher va rumba rumba rum.

The song became a class favorite, not so much because it was part of a recent history in which some of our parents had been involved, but because it transported us to mysterious Africa. We liked singing it in a circle and clapping our hands in time, imagining ourselves a group of tribesmen chanting around a camp fire.

My third year at school marked the end of informality and the beginning of a tough impersonal routine. Friends were no longer Shoshana, Yair, or Aharon but Brusnawitzky, Greenberg, and Kroll. We had a strict timetable and a different master for each subject. Even the names of the subjects had changed. Sums became mathematics, knowledge of the country became geography, story time became history, and reading became literature. My father took my form for biology and taught us to anesthetize and dissect frogs caught the night before in the school's frog garden.

In spite of increasing homework and frequent tests, there was plenty of time to romp about and most afternoons some of us would reassemble on the school grounds for a game of hide-and-seek or catch-as-catch-can. I was about to return home one evening when I realized with a sinking heart that I had dropped my latchkey somewhere on the grounds. Everybody joined in the search. It was practically dark when a thin boy with a pointed chin and an intelligent face triumphantly retrieved it from under a small bush where I had been hiding earlier. The boy's name was Ephraim but we called him Eppi; at the time of writing he is Israel's ambassador to the United States.

One evening I returned home from a hide-and-seek game with a violent headache. A primus stove was burning in my head, its unbearable din mounting and receding in regular cycles. I kept mumbling that my mother's head looked like a three-story house. The family lady doctor diagnosed typhus and I was rushed to the Hadassa Hospital, the only building in the neighborhood with green shutters instead of the common light brown.

I was never told how long I had been delirious, but one day I woke up and asked the nurse, "What's that red card attached to my bed?"

"You've been very ill."

"What's your name?"

"Just call me sister."

Hospital nurses, whatever their rank in the medical hierarchy, were called merciful sisters, probably a Hebrew rendering of Sisters of Mercy; usage has since dropped the merciful. I could not bring myself to call a strange woman sister, so I did not call her anything, and since I was unable to attract her attention when I wanted to, I earned a reputation for being an undemanding patient.

I was in a children's ward. There was one sweet little boy

who kept coughing and another who kept crying for his Mummy. There were no screens to put around the cots and whenever we felt the urge we sat on our chamber pots in full view. I saw Sister wash Asaf in a small portable bath, stand him on a table, and hold a test tube to his penis.

"He's giving me a specimen," she explained.

Some time later Asaf was put again on the table, his pajama top taken off, and cupping glasses applied to his back. I watched, speechless with horror, as his skin rose under the suction like so many mounds. Sister laughed.

Now that I was better I was conscious of my parents visiting me. Their visits were my only distraction; I was not allowed library books for fear I might contaminate them. On one of his visits my father produced a sheaf of papers closely covered with his tiny handwriting.

"I'm going to read it to you," he said.

He read me his own translation from the German of Johanna Spyri's *Heidi*. Every time he came to see me he had another chapter ready for me. By the time I was allowed home I had been read the whole book. An authorized translation into Hebrew was not published until several years later.

When I returned home I noticed that father was not there.

"Dad has taken a room in Pevsner's House," mother said. "He has a lot of work to do and there isn't enough peace and quiet for him here."

I went around to see him. He had rented a low-ceilinged room on the ground floor of a fortress-like house, with its own entrance through a shrub-lined path. It was a cool room, dark, with lots of books on the floor and the microscope on the desk. I told father I had decided to become a writer.

"It calls for perseverance," he warned. "Remember the Talmudic saying: *Neglect it but a day and it will neglect you for two.*"

"I'll persevere," I promised.

After that father made a habit of coming by Shapira's House to take me out for an evening walk. He did not come in but stopped outside the front gate and gave the family whistle, the one that used to bring old Zariz bounding.

"Dad is whistling for you," mother would say. Something in her voice made me feel guilty.

"What have you two been doing with yourselves?" she asked one evening when I had returned.

"Just walked around."

"Didn't he take you visiting?"

"N-no."

"He didn't take you to Mrs. Haskell's?"

"No, no."

"Are you sure?"

"Quite sure," I lied. Mrs. Haskell was an American widow newly arrived from New York with her schoolboy son. I had rather enjoyed our meeting, for since I left Bat Galim and the Holmses there was no one to speak English with. I felt guiltier than ever.

One afternoon a classmate named Eli came to play. He wandered from one room to another and demanded to be told where everybody slept.

"I sleep here," I pointed to a bed in a small room. "And my mother sleeps in the bed opposite."

"And your brother and sister?"

I showed him.

"And your father?"

"In his study in Pevsner's House. There isn't enough peace and quiet here for his work."

Eli gave me a shrewd look. "Nonsense," he said. "There's been a divorce."

The word went through me like a dagger. I had seen it in books but it was the first time I heard it spoken. I had nothing to say.

After Eli had left I picked up a children's magazine and started turning the pages. A black-and-white reproduction of a portrait caught my eye. A pretty little girl was sitting in a wood, her short hair caught in a band, her hands clasped to her heart, and her bare toes peeping from under her wide skirt. She had a trusting face, as only the face of a child who had never been hurt can be. The caption said it was *The Age of Innocence* by Sir Joshua Reynolds.

I was still gazing at the picture when it dawned on me that this was an age I was inexorably growing out of, perhaps had already grown out of, and I began to weep for the end of innocence and the passing of what I sensed had been the happiest part of my childhood. I was eight years old.

PART TWO
A New World

I called the new world into existence,
to redress the balance of the old.

George Canning, 1770–1827

9

First Glimpse of the Palestine Triangle

IT WAS SIESTA TIME for the adults. My seventeen-year-old sister, who was not yet an adult but no longer a child, was rummaging in the drawers of mother's desk.

"I'm running away to a kibbutz," she whispered when I looked up from my book. "Don't wake Mum up. I've left a note."

She slipped into her pocket the few shillings she had found in a drawer and tiptoed out clutching a toothbrush. I went back to my reading. It never occurred to me to question my sister's action or disobey her instructions.

The day before she and my mother had had an argument. My sister had just come home from her Tel Aviv school for the summer holidays and announced that she was a member of a newly formed ideological circle whose belief was that the country had too many intellectuals and too few agricultural laborers. The young members, most of whom came from the upper forms of the Herzlia Gymnasium, proposed to interrupt their schooling and found their own kibbutz.

"You want to work on a kibbutz?" mother had said incredulously.

"That's right."

"I don't believe it. It's just an excuse to shirk exams."

"Hard work on a kibbutz is more important than exams."

"You have no idea what hard work is," mother had

shouted angrily. "You've never done a stroke of hard work in your life. You always leave the washing up to others."

My sister later admitted that the rebuke had cut to the quick and decided her there and then to prove that she could work as hard as anybody. The day following the argument she caught the narrow-gauge train from Haifa to the Valley of Jezreel and got off at Geva, a small kibbutz founded in 1921. Near the barn she saw a group of holiday volunteers from a Tel Aviv school and pretended to be one of them. She was sent to work in the tomato field.

At home her rebellion had gone entirely unchallenged. Mother sent after her a bagful of working clothes and father, pretending to be passing through Geva on one of his hikes, stopped by the tomato field to give his daughter a tip or two. A few weeks later mother and I caught the same narrow-gauge train to see Geva for ourselves. We were taken to an oak wood by the spring of Harod and I spent a happy day walking barefoot and flinging stones into the water. At the end of the summer holidays my sister went back to school and the following year took her matriculation examination.

But the idea of setting up a new kibbutz had not been an adolescent whim. No sooner had the young members taken their school exams than they left Tel Aviv to work on the land. The plan was to get some practical experience while seeking financial support for starting on their own. Ten of them, including my sister, went to Hadera, roughly halfway between Haifa and Tel Aviv, and offered themselves as daily laborers to the well-to-do orange growers of the village.

Hadera, today a town with a population of some 35,000, was founded in 1890 as an agricultural settlement in a swampy, mosquito-infested area, and the original settlers had to contend with malaria as well as with Arab attacks. Baron Rothschild came to the rescue and sent for Egyptian workmen to lay out a drainage system. At the same time thousands of swamp-draining eucalyptus trees were planted, and in 1929, when my sister arrived there, malaria was under control, though not altogether eradicated.

The young people lived in a ramshackle hut on top of a hill, washed under an outdoor tap, and shared their bread and soup with another group of idealists. During the orange season my sister carried a ladder, leaned it against a tree, and climbed up to pick the fruit. When the season was over she was sent to work on the road which was going to join the village to the railway station. By day she chopped stones into gravel, by night she took part in heated arguments about building a new society based on socialism and equality. Before long she caught malaria. After several bouts she was forbidden any more work and was sent to convalesce in the new sanatorium of Moza, near Jerusalem. For the first few days she was so weak she could hardly bring herself to obey the bell calling convalescents for meals.

That was at the beginning of August. Before the month was out she was caught up in a wave of Arab violence which had swept most of the country.

The *casus belli* for the 1929 disturbances was an Arab claim that the Jews were encroaching on the traditional Muslim place of worship near the Western Wall in Jerusalem and had designs on other Muslim holy places as well. On August 23 an Arab mob attacked Jews in Jerusalem, daily renewing their attacks until driven back by members of a secret Jewish organization called *Hagana*, Defense. On August 24 seventy Jews were slaughtered in Hebron, and the rest, all descendants of the ancient Jewish community, were evacuated to Jerusalem. Safed too suffered casualties and several villages near Jerusalem were attacked and burned. Moza was one of them.

The Moza convalescent home had been built on a high hill in order to give patients the best of the mountain air and was therefore some distance from the village. One morning—my sister remembered it as being a Saturday—shooting was heard from the direction of the village for several hours. At midday a string of refugees was seen walking up the hill, women carrying young children, old men carrying sticks and hatchets. When they reached the comparative safety of the convalescent home they reported that some of the Moza settlers had been killed and their houses set on fire. The few able-bodied men left had decided to hold out as long as they could.

The isolated convalescent home was an obvious target and both inmates and refugees were herded upstairs to the second floor and ordered to take cover under the beds. Some members of Hagana arrived to defend the place, but their entire weaponry consisted of two rifles and three pistols. They discreetly disappeared when a British armored car with policemen drove up, shortly to be reinforced by British soldiers dispatched from their base in Egypt. The siege lasted several days, with bullets shrieking overhead and ricocheting off the walls. A ball of fire brushed my sister's arm but left her unharmed. Like the rest of the inmates, she took turns in keeping watch and passing messages from the lookout post on the roof to the operational headquarters on the ground floor. Every now and then she reported flames leaping up from the village below and the soldiers rushed down to put them out. Once they brought back a seventeen-year-old lad, only a year younger than herself, with severe stab wounds in the head, chest, arms, and legs. When he regained consciousness he began telling my sister what he had been through.

The British machine guns eventually drove off the Arab attackers, but the soldiers, to the inmates' indignation, refused to take sides; they regarded the whole affray as just another military assignment. In vain did my sister and her friends try to expound the ideological background of the conflict and win the British army over to the cause of the *yishuv*, the Jewish population of Palestine. The soldiers listened politely enough but whenever asked what they thought they just leered at the girls and said, "Are you married?"

"None of your business."

"Will you marry me?"

"Go to hell."

"That's gratitude for you."

The British army was unanimously dismissed as ignorant and obtuse.

While this was happening at Moza, an Arab attack was also attempted on the Jewish suburbs of Haifa. In the morning I went to school as usual. At sunset about half a dozen strangers were standing on the crescent-shaped veranda of our apartment and anxiously looking towards the Arab Old City below, barely a mile away. A few bangs went off. They sounded just like the familiar *warda barood*, only there had been no warning cries.

"What was that?" I inquired.

"Nothing to worry about. Some wicked people are trying to make trouble." Mother said "people," not "Arabs."

The attack was repelled by Hagana, and so was an attack on Tel Aviv. When law and order were restored my mother asked me what I made of the recent events; she had seen me trying to read *Ha'aretz*, the daily paper taken at home.

"The paper says the Arabs want Palestine for themselves," I told her, reporting what I had read.

"How do you know it does not really belong to them?"

The answer seemed so obvious I was surprised she had bothered to ask. Perhaps mother was not aware that the stories of the Bible formed an important part of my schoolwork.

"Of course it doesn't," I said with unshakable conviction. "The Bible says that God gave the Land of Israel to Abraham and his seed. We are Abraham's seed. The country is ours."

I then learned to my great bewilderment that God's

promise to Abraham was not considered binding in the modern era and that it had taken the Balfour Declaration to reaffirm the ancient Jewish right to the Promised Land.

Until then Balfour had been just another of those foreign names by which some of Haifa's streets were known: Herzl Street, Nordau Street, Pevsner Street, Balfour Street. Now I heard that Balfour was a great Englishman who had been inspired by God to try to save Jews all over the world from persecution and the disgrace of exile.

The declaration had been given only twelve years earlier, in 1917, and its promise of a national home for the Jewish people in Palestine was to be quoted so often within my hearing that the words became engraved on my heart like the Ten Commandments. I thought of Balfour as one of the Thirty-six Righteous Men whom God plants among mankind at any given time and imagined him standing on a raised wooden platform in a large amphitheater, unrolling the declaration in full view and reading it out to thousands of cheering Englishmen who, as everybody knew, were brought up on the Bible and therefore aware of God's promise to Abraham. When, several years later, my history master happened to mention that the declaration had been made in the form of a brief letter to Lord Lionel Walter Rothschild, as from a British Foreign Secretary to the lay head of British Jewry, I found it difficult to accept.

Orator or not, Balfour was our latter-day prophet. A village founded in 1922 in the Valley of Jezreel was named Balfouria; a project of afforestation materialized into the Balfour Forest; Hadar Hacarmel's widest road was called Balfour Street; and patriotic parents named their baby boys Balfour. November 2, the anniversary of the declaration, was a day of national celebration observed by public meetings, articles in the press, festive dinners, and all but a day off from school, which was unfair and just went to show that adults had a wrong sense of values.

After the 1929 disturbances I tried to keep up my laborious reading of an adult paper. Students of Hebrew will know that while it is relatively easy to read a text which has the vowel signs printed in full, it is quite difficult to read one which leaves most of them out. Adult newspapers, unlike children's books and magazines, were printed without vowel signs, and understanding them required greater expertise than I had at the time. It was not only a question of deciding, according to context, whether a combination of consonants such as *sfr* was to be read *sefer*, *safar*, *sappar*, or *sipper*, each reading conveying a different meaning; there was also the strange adult vocabulary. I was particularly mystified by the recurring reference to something called *hasefer halavan*, literally meaning the White Book. Nobody thought to tell me that this was the Hebrew way of referring to the White Paper, a British government statement of policy presented to Parliament.

The policy statement which the daily press angrily commented on at the time was the Passfield White Paper of 1930. It gave me my first introduction to the complexities of the Arab-Jewish conflict and Britain's part in it.

Before the First World War Britain was the only great power which had shown sympathy for Zionist aspirations in a practical form. In 1902 it considered a request from Herzl for facilities for Jewish colonization at El Arish in the Sinai Peninsula, and in 1903 it offered him a chance to set up an autonomous Jewish settlement in British East Africa. The Balfour Declaration in 1917 was a British recognition of the Jewish national aspirations in Palestine. At the same time the declaration safeguarded the rights of the Arabs. The full text, which has remained a bitter bone of contention ever since, ran as follows:

His Majesty's Government view with favour the establishment in Palestine of a national home for the Jewish people, and will use their best endeavour to facilitate the achievement of this ob-

- 97 -

ject, it being clearly understood that nothing shall be done which may prejudice the civil and religious rights of existing non-Jewish communities in Palestine, or the rights and political status enjoyed by Jews in any other country.*

The Arab leaders correctly interpreted the declaration as a blow to their own national aspirations and called for resistance. The first British High Commissioner to Palestine had not yet taken up his post when a wave of Arab violence swept the country in the spring of 1920, culminating in the destruction of Tel Hai, a small settlement in Upper Galilee. Two years later the first of six White Papers was issued, setting a pattern which became characteristic of the entire span of the British mandate in Palestine: an outburst of violence, British re-thinking of policy, and a White Paper.

The 1922 White Paper bore the name of Winston Churchill, then Secretary of State for the Colonies. He reaffirmed that the Balfour Declaration was not subject to modifications and that the Jews were in Palestine as of right. At the same time he conceded that there was no question of allowing Palestine to become overwhelmingly Jewish and introduced a system of immigration quota based on the economic absorptive capacity of the country as a whole.

The next White Paper came out in 1930, as the result of the 1929 Arab violence, and bore the name of Lord Passfield, the new Secretary of State for the Colonies. That was my first "White Book." Struggling slowly with the non-vowelled text of the daily newspaper, I managed to get the gist of the two main recommendations: Jewish immigration was to be curbed, and land purchase from the Arabs was to be restricted. Wherever I went I heard

*From the letter written by Arthur James Balfour to Lord Rothschild, dated Foreign Office, November 2, 1917, now at the British Museum.

people indignantly discussing the Passfield White Paper; at the lending library, at the greengrocer's, on street corners. I too was indignant. I could not understand why Jews, who were known to be hard-working and in need of a national home, were not allowed to return freely to their own ancient country, and I could not see why wealthy Arab landowners, who felt like selling their swampy acres to Jews for a good price, were debarred from so doing.

The Passfield White Paper was not implemented and in 1931 was more or less allowed to lapse. People around me were relieved and I felt free to drop the hard labor of deciphering an adult newspaper and return to the world of fantasy, devouring the smooth-flowing translations of Walter Scott's *Ivanhoe* and *The Talisman*. I was not at all surprised that the stories were set in such places as Jerusalem and En Gedi; the Holy Land, I knew, was the center of the universe.

My brief foray into adult newspapers had left me with a puzzle. In Hebrew the word for colony is *moshava*, which also means village. Lord Passfield, who was Secretary for the Colonies, appeared to an inexperienced reader like me to be Secretary for the Villages. I wondered for a long time why Great Britain should have appointed a Secretary to look after our villages which, like Hadera, were fairly prosperous, and not after our kibbutzim which, like Geva, were very poor and in much greater need of being looked after.

10

British and American

THE OFFICIAL NAME of the country was Palestine in English and Arabic, and Palestina (EI) in Hebrew, the letters in parentheses being the initials of the historic Hebrew name Eretz Israel, the Land of Israel. For us the two names were synonymous. We called ourselves Eretz Israelis when speaking Hebrew and Palestinians when speaking any other language.

We were proud of being Palestinian and could easily tell who was and who was not. Mr. Klein, a Polish-born music teacher, was Palestinian; Abdallah the vegetable vendor, who had acquired some Russian and his Christianity at the Carmelite convent school on the French Carmel, was Palestinian; but mother's lodger Monsieur Armand, who ran a mysterious business in the Old City and often traveled to Damascus, was not. He was Syrian.

I already knew that if you wanted to travel you had to have a passport. I had taken a good look at my sister's when she had given up working on a kibbutz and was about to leave for Vienna to study modern ballet. The words "British Passport" were embossed in gold over the brown cover, just above the royal coat of arms with the legends *Honi soit qui mal y pense* and *Dieu et mon droit*. The passport had been issued "by His Britannic Majesty's High Commissioner for Palestine" and the information was repeated in each of the three official languages, with the Hebrew text duly including the parenthesized EI.

"His Britannic Majesty" read like something out of Sir Walter Scott's stories of the Crusades. For some unaccountable reason the words led me to believe that Britain was a country which bred tall people, and I was not surprised when a knowledgeable classmate informed me that members of the British Police Force in Palestine were six foot tall to a man. Six feet, I calculated, was the equivalent of 180 centimeters.

Conversions of weights and measures, like chewing gum and Players cigarettes, had come in with the British and were a hated part of my schoolwork. I had just returned to my classroom from the annual medical checkup when my math master said, "How tall are you now?"

"Eighty centimeters," I answered meekly, for I was one of the youngest in class and small for my age at that.

"And how much do you weigh?"

"Twenty-one kilos and two hundred and seventy-five grams."

"Good girl. Now convert it into English measures and weights."

And so we toiled to convert an easy metric system into inches, feet, and yards, as well as pounds, ounces, stone, gallons, miles, and acres. To add to the confusion, the metric system was by no means the only one in use. While personal weight was measured in kilograms and grams, foodstuffs were weighed by the *rotel* and the *okia*. Even then there was no uniformity. In Jerusalem a *rotel* was divided into twelve *okias*, in Haifa into ten.

"Why do we have to convert centimeters into inches?" I ventured to ask one day. "The dressmaker takes my measurements in centimeters."

"We are governed by Britain," I was gravely told. "Conversions will help you understand how the English think."

Another importation from Britain was the movement of boy scouts and girl guides. The Reali School was very keen on scouting and most of my form joined the Cubs and

Brownies. There was much talk of good citizenship, the daily good turn and the need to obtain proficiency badges. Every afternoon one patrol or another assembled on the school grounds for the weekly activity.

I was anxious to do well in my proficiency test and diligently practiced all the required skills. I was able to tie a perfect weaver's knot, although I did not know what to do with it once I had tied it and privately believed that weavers were evil creatures who belonged in the Brothers Grimm's fairy tales. I was equally dubious about the practical application of a sailor's knot, since I knew better than most that sailors did not tie their boats to rocks but carried them to a safe hiding place among the sand dunes. Learning how to light a camp fire made more sense, and making improvised stretchers was fun. I spent long afternoons blowing shrill Morse code messages on my whistle while my brother, more advanced in scouting hierarchy, exchanged semaphore signs with his chums on the school's disused tennis court.

We were required to know about Baden-Powell and the siege of Mafeking although I, for one, was not quite sure where Mafeking was. We also had to make ourselves familiar with the history of Zionism. Dr. Theodor Herzl, I memorized, was really Dr. Benjamin Zeev Herzl. He was born in 1860 in Budapest—where was Budapest anyway?—and would have ended as he had begun, an Assimilated Jew, had his eyes not been opened to the danger of anti-Semitism by the Dreyfus case in France. He then conceived the idea of a national home for the Jews in Palestine and embodied it in a novel called *Altneuland* in German and *Tel Aviv*, Hill of Spring, in the Hebrew translation.

Another set piece concerned the origin of the Blue Box, the popular name for a collection box issued to schools by the Jewish National Fund. It was Professor Hermann Zvi Schapira, I memorized, a rabbi turned mathematician, who in 1901 launched the idea of a Jewish National Fund which would buy land from Arabs in Palestine and lease it indefinitely to Jewish settlers.

As far as I understood the finances of the Jewish National Fund, they depended entirely on the generosity and dedication of schoolchildren. Every classroom had a blue collection box with a map of Palestine drawn over it in white, and we were constantly urged to drop through the slot as many coppers or half-piasters as we had been able to extort from our parents. On Friday the contributions were added up and the form whose blue box had yielded the highest total won an honorable mention. The weekly ceremony ended with a song exhorting people to redeem more land. Buying land from the Arabs was never referred to as buying; it was always redeeming.

In the summer Cubs and Brownies were taken camping on Mount Carmel. I learned to put up a ridge tent and was taught to encircle it with limestone to keep scorpions out. A Cub in the tent opposite was about to pull on his boots when a patrol leader yelled out, "Stop, stop!"

"What's the matter?"

"Shake your boots out first, you fool! Don't you know about scorpions?"

We had to be constantly on the alert, even at home. One chilly autumn evening I went to the wicker case where winter clothes were stored in mothballs to pull out mother's black woolen shawl. The light in the room was dim, and as I pushed the lid back I could just about distinguish the shawl with its black tufts right on top of the pile. I do not know what instinct made me suspicious of one particular tuft and stopped me picking up the shawl. Sure enough, it was a scorpion.

Autumn was followed by winter, one of the few winters I remember from that period. There was a paraffin stove to keep the room warm, and a boiling kettle over it to keep the air humid. The room was stuffy. The paraffin had run out and the wick gave out a disagreeable smell. There were five of us around: my brother, myself, our two American boarders Bernie and Anna, and the young woman who was paid to see that we did our homework while mother was out at work. Bernie, who was burly and confident, said he could fix the stove and started messing about with the wick. My brother tried to push Bernie out of the way in order to have a go on his own. Little Anna and I crowded around to see who was winning and the young woman screamed that we were setting the house on fire. The flames leaped up high, bursting out from all sides of the stove, then subsided to give way to a thick column of soot. The young woman burst into tears and we wondered why she was making such a fuss over what was clearly good clean fun.

Bernie and his two sisters had at first lived with their mother on the floor above us. The mother was heavily built and matronly, her eldest daughter pale and lank, Bernie thick-set and always looking as if about to charge, and little Anna sweet but rather willful. None of them had any Hebrew to speak of and the air rang with their uninhibited American twang. Anna was younger than I and whenever she refused to follow my lead I would say ponderously, "I don't like Anna."

"Yes you do."

"No I don't."

There would be a flood of tears and little Anna would then do whatever I thought she ought to have done in the first place.

They came to board with us after an accident which might well have cost them their lives. The mother and her three children were admiring the sea view from their second-floor balcony when it suddenly collapsed, stone railings and human bodies crashing heavily into the garden below. The mother had her collarbone and several ribs fractured, Bernie was bruised, only the two girls escaped unhurt. Bernie and Anna were left with us until the end of term, when they rejoined their convalescent mother in the States.

There were many American children at the Reali School at that time, sent over by their Zionist parents to be educated in Palestine for a year or two. Most of them lived at the school boarding house and led a supervised existence which to the rest of us seemed unnatural and unenviable. They were distinguishable from a distance by their bright-colored shirts and jumpers, their way of carrying their schoolbooks loose in their arms instead of satchels and, on acquaintance, by such outlandish names as Phyllis, Leonard, or Oscar.

Oscar was a classmate. He was as tall as I was short, but since I was a good runner I was often matched against him in mixed relay races. He had thick dark hair, brown eyes, and a broken front tooth. I was passing my tongue over my own broken front tooth when I suddenly knew that I was in love.

There followed an exciting exchange of notes surreptitiously passed during lessons from desk to desk by eager accomplices, until our love became an accepted fact of school life. At the end of the summer term Oscar returned to the States and we started writing to each other, at first in Hebrew but gradually, as Oscar began to forget what little Hebrew he had known, in English.

A year or two passed. One morning the postman left a form notifying me that there was a parcel bearing my name at the Customs House in the Old City and that on production of satisfactory evidence of identity it might be surrendered to me subject to His Majesty's Customs and Excise regulations. Going to the Customs House was an adult business which required not only ample time but also a knack for arguing with officials. Mother said she could not take a day off work to chase up some silly present that Oscar had taken into his head to send me from America, but my sister took pity on me and found time to release the parcel from bondage. It contained a silver-plated bracelet engraved with my initials and a date. I stared with astonishment, unfamiliar as I was with the American way of putting month before day, at a set of figures which suggested that my current birthday fell on the 4th day of the 19th month of the year 1934. My brother said that the bracelet looked like a dog collar. I still have it.

The correspondence eventually petered out, but the story has a sequel. Towards the end of the Second World War my father, who had been Oscar's form master, had a letter from him. Oscar wrote that he was serving with the American forces somewhere in Europe and that he was married. "Your daughter might like to know," he concluded, "that my wife's name is Ruth."

My mother and I were now living on our own in what must have been one of the first modern blocks of flats in Haifa. It was a four-story monster of a building divided into two wings, with eight flats to each wing. There were no trees and no flower beds; instead there were communal clotheslines and dustbins. The flats were identical and the hallway had a list of rules posted on the wall. There was a Babel of languages. Mrs. Donsky spoke Russian, Mrs. Sachs spoke German, Mrs. Wiseman spoke English, Mrs. Azaria spoke Hebrew. The block, unnumbered of course, was known as Lurie's House after its American owner. Mr. and Mrs. Lurie did not live on the premises but called from time to time to inspect the property. Since they did not speak Hebrew and most of the tenants could not speak English, they communicated in Yiddish. Mother said that Mrs. Lurie spoke the most beautiful Yiddish she had ever heard. I still regarded Yiddish as a bastard language and was amazed to hear it associated with beauty.

My father too had moved. He had taken a room in Mrs.

Haskell's spacious apartment and after a while my brother moved in to share a room with her son who was a classmate of his. Because nobody said anything to me about the domestic setup I did not realize for a long time that my father had remarried. I thought that both he and my brother were lodgers at Mrs. Haskell's, like the lodgers my mother took in to supplement her earnings. Mrs. Haskell continued to be known by that name and at school, where she was a part-time teacher of English, nobody ever referred to her by any other. I made a habit of calling on father and her several times a week, not so much for their company as for that of their spaniel and another pet, of whom more later. Mother made no attempt to stop me.

Mrs. Haskell's apartment was the most elegant I had ever seen, containing items of furniture I had never known to exist. There was a bureau with a bookcase to match, a gateleg table, an oval dining table with six upholstered chairs, a gramophone in a solid wooden case, embroidered drapings, and rugs to cover the stone-tiled floors. There was also a collection of silverware on display with a tower-like filigree object whose purpose I could not make out. Mrs. Haskell, deeply shocked, told me it was used for the *havdala*, a religious ritual performed at the conclusion of the Sabbath.

"Like father like daughter," she sighed.

She and father did not see eye to eye about religious observance. Mrs. Haskell liked to keep what was known as "a good Jewish household," while father had no use for even the most lukewarm form of religious practice. One Friday afternoon I found her red-eyed and father sullen. They had had a fierce argument about his plans for the Sabbath. He had arranged to lead a hike, but Mrs. Haskell insisted that he should stay at home and preside over the festive Friday dinner and ritual. She had cried, and argued, and begged so much that in the end he gave in; and rather bizarre he looked that evening, sitting at table with a borrowed black cap on, crossly hurrying through the prescribed text in the prayer book.

But Mrs. Haskell's triumph was short-lived. At about midnight, when the rest of the household was fast asleep, father pulled on his hobnailed boots and pith helmet and quietly slipped out of the house to march throughout the night and catch up with his hikers at whatever mountain pass they had camped the evening before. After that a domestic compromise was worked out, allowing father to alternate between a weekend hike and a Sabbath at home.

One of the attractions of a visit to my father's was Mrs. Haskell's delicious homemade pastries. She always offered me some but I, who had absorbed the oriental notion that accepting with alacrity was a sign of ill breeding, invariably declined. A hostess who knew the etiquette would press the pastries on her guest again and again, knowing that only the third offering could be accepted without violating conventions, but Mrs. Haskell, who had been born and bred in New York, did not play the game according to the rules. She allowed me to go pastryless and frustrated. Sometimes, when she left the room, I would swiftly scoop some into my mouth and try to look innocent when she returned. She must have noticed how sparse the pastry plate looked after each of my visits, for one day, when I declined her offer as usual, she taught me a new rule: "There is no virtue in saying no when you mean yes. If you want some pastries say yes please and help yourself." It was a revelation.

By New York standards I was a savage and Mrs. Haskell took it upon herself to civilize me. She subjected me to long sermons on good manners and social behavior and assured me that it was a matter of hygiene, not vanity, to keep my fingernails trimmed. She was flabbergasted when I told her that I had never had a bath in my life and that a daily shower, usually cold, was quite adequate. To prove me wrong she rubbed my neck with absorbent cotton dipped in surgical spirit and showed me how grubby it was. I was terribly embarrassed but did not deviate from the view that bathing was a decadent habit, practiced by the ancient Romans before their fall and later copied by an effete Western civilization.

Mrs. Haskell talked to me in English—her Hebrew was virtually nonexistent—and smiled indulgently when I remarked that my old chums at Bat Galim had pronounced things differently. Father wanted me to call her Aunt Fanny and Aunt Fanny expected me to kiss her whenever I came to see her. I did not think her attractive except once, when she undid her severe bun and let her glorious black hair cascade freely over her shoulders. As time went by I grew very fond of her, recognizing that she was kind, tolerant, and always ready to help.

Here I must anticipate. One day I called as usual and was told that Mrs. Haskell was ill. I took little notice and went downstairs to see my classmate Zephyra who lived on the floor below. The following morning I saw Zephyra in the school corridor just before first bell and was surprised when she did not return my cheerful greeting.

"What's the matter?" I asked.

"Haven't you heard?"

"Heard what?"

She then told me that Mrs. Haskell had died during the night.

The first period that morning was Hebrew literature. I asked to be excused and was wandering aimlessly down the corridor when my Arabic master noticed me and asked solicitously, "How is Mummy?"

His blunder made me choke. It was impossible, as well as futile, to try to explain that my mother was well but that Mrs. Haskell, who was my father's wife, was dead. I rushed past him into the cloakroom and burst into uncontrollable sobs, pretending to blow my nose whenever I heard someone walk in.

The funeral was terrible. Father, unrecognizable in a suit and felt hat instead of khaki drill and pith helmet, looked lost. A crowd of mourners walked silently behind the coffin while strange men in black kaftans, black hats, and black side curls energetically rattled collection boxes and demanded alms in loud persistent voices. They were the functionaries of the Jewish burial society who had already been paid a high fee for their exclusive right to bury the dead and were now pestering the mourners to give money to an unspecified religious cause. They clung like leeches. I wanted to hit them. They had nothing to do with Mrs. Haskell, my father, or grief. When I got home to mother I refused lunch and shut myself in the W.C. to cry over the irrevocability of death and the exploitation of bereavement in the name of religion.

II

Bo-Kah

MY FATHER was the sort of person to whom total strangers from all over the country took any wild animal, bird, or reptile they happened to have captured. He kept his pets in an enclosure adjoining the school biology room and allowed none but his most trusted senior pupils to look after them. At different times he kept deer, a weasel, a badger, a mongoose, a pair of loving quails, eagles, and once, for a brief spell, a skunk.

One summer day a tough-looking fellow knocked at Mrs. Haskell's front door and asked to see "the teacher who takes in beasts."

"Got something for you here," he mumbled. "Keep it if y'like."

He undid his rucksack and pulled out a frightened little cub which he said he had found bleating pitifully in a lonely ravine on the Carmel range. The cub was gray with black stripes running along its body and around its haunches. When father made it stand, its front legs were longer than its hind ones.

"Wild cat?" the fellow ventured.

"A hyena," father said excitedly. The fellow snatched his rucksack and bolted.

Father decided to try to bring up the hyena like a household pet. He put it in a small iron cage borrowed from the school storeroom and kept it in his bedroom *cum* study. For two days the cub bleated and wailed until it dropped off into an exhausted sleep, only to wake up and start all over again. On the third day it accepted several saucerfuls of milk and began watching father with what looked like an intelligent interest. Father opened the cage.

"Come and get it," he cajoled, holding out a lump of sugar.

The little hyena loved the taste of sugar and did not take long to work out the connection between cause and effect. No sooner would father utter the magic words than the cub would happily rush out to claim its reward. It became so adept at obeying the call that *bo kah*, the Hebrew for Come-and-get-it, became its official name.

From the very first day Bo-Kah showed high regard for cleanliness. He did not foul his cage and after very few reprimands stopped fouling father's room as well, waiting instead to be let out into the yard, where the mixture of earth and pebbles was much to his liking. He was about four weeks old when he came into our life. At three months he had taught himself the trick of reaching with his teeth for the door handle in father's room and pulling it down to let himself out. At that stage Mrs. Haskell said that although Bo-Kah was a honey she could not allow a grown hyena to wander freely about the place; her daily help was nervous and was threatening to give notice.

There was an old olive tree growing in the middle of the yard, with its trunk deeply hollowed. Father thought it might serve as a den. He bought a long iron chain and fastened one end to a stake near the tree and the other to a collar inscribed with Bo-Kah's name and address. Bo-Kah, who had never been collared and chained before, was disgruntled.

"*Bo kah*," father said invitingly, leaving some lumps of sugar in the hollow.

Bo-kah brightened up. After he had crunched the lumps of sugar and accepted that no more were coming his way, he gave the hollow a thorough sniff and found it to his liking. Next thing we knew he was energetically digging inside with his front paws, kicking the spare soil back with his hind legs. Father had to remove several bucketfuls of soil before Bo-Kah was satisfied that his den was deep enough. After that he stationed himself at the entrance and eyed everyone who walked into the house liked a trained security officer. He was quiet enough by day, for people stopped to talk to him, but at night, when darkness made him invisible, he felt neglected. As soon as he heard the yard gate open, he uttered a joyful cry and rushed forward like an eager dog. Neighbors from the other three apartments grew accustomed to his voice and returned his greeting in the dark, but visitors could only discern a pair of fearfully glinting eyes and ran away in panic. Bo-Kah's chain was of course well short of the path and he could not molest anybody even if he had a mind to.

He grew up quite harmless, giving the lie to the notions commonly held about his kind. A hyena was believed to be cruel and bloodthirsty, a haunter of cemeteries, a digger of graves, and an eater of corpses. Bo-Kah enjoyed fresh fruit and rice pudding. Superstition had it that a hyena could turn a dog deaf and blind by merely casting his shadow over it. Bo-Kah rather liked Kushi the spaniel and gallantly—though unsuccessfully, because he was heavy on his feet—tried to help her chase cats. Arab peasants claimed that a hyena's nighttime laughter drove people crazy. Bo-Kah managed to modulate his grating bleat into something like a loving purr whenever he heard father's footsteps. As time went by we found him more intelligent than Kushi, more sociable, and more consistent in his ways.

At first he was kept to a vegetarian diet. He ate bread, cheese, bananas, oranges, watermelons, grapes, and once, when nobody was watching, the leather straps off father's slippers and rucksack. After that he was offered his first taste of meat. Bo-Kah was beside himself with excitement.

He groaned and moaned, swallowed and choked, vomited and started all over again. Soon afterwards he saw three hens strolling in the yard within reach of his chain and killed them before anybody could stop him, finishing one off and storing the other two in his den for later. His favorite dish, however, was rice pudding. When father experimentally offered him a bowl of rice pudding together with a bowl of meat, Bo-Kah took only one bite of the meat and turned to the pudding, allowing Kushi to clean up what he had spurned. He knew exactly what he liked. When I mistakenly offered him savory rice instead of rice pudding he disgustedly kicked the bowl away, then picked it up with his teeth and placed it face down as far away from his den as his chain would allow.

My own great treat was to accompany father when he took his pets for their evening walk. Kushi was allowed to run free while Bo-Kah was led, straining fiercely to keep up with her. In the end he too was let loose and the two animals ran joyfully along, Kushi gracefully sprinting backwards and forwards, Bo-Kah heavily lumbering behind. Sometimes we took them to the Arab end of Hadar Hacarmel, where there was something like a field. Several Arab youths began following us one evening.

"By *Allah*, what a dog," a voice said behind us.

"It's not a dog," came another voice.

"By *Allah* it is. It's an American dog."

The youths overtook us and confronted father.

"*Ya hawaja*, sir," they said ingratiatingly. "This dog of yours, not the black one, the one with the stripes, is it an American dog?"

"It's a hyena," I said importantly.

They took no notice of me. Women were of no account. "*Ya hawaja*," they repeated. "What is it?"

"It's a *debba* like the girl said."

At that moment Bo-Kah decided to confirm his master's assertion and treated his audience to a sample of his raucous nighttime laughter. The youths vanished as if by magic and a moment later stones began to ricochet around us.

"Abu Hassan," distant voices called. *"Abu Hassan!"*

The youths' reaction was predictable, based as it was on age-old tradition. Local folklore had it that a young Arab lad named Hassan was returning to his village late one night when a hyena crossed his path and fixed him with its green glinting eyes. Hassan was petrified. The hyena raised itself on its hind legs and pounded with its front paws on Hassan's chest, forcing him back step by step. In vain did Hassan call out *"Abuya, abuya*—father, father"; not even his father dared come to the rescue. When the hyena had forced Hassan back as far as its den, it cracked his skull with its teeth and ate its fill of him, burying the rest for the following day. Ever since then a hyena was known as *Abu Hassan,* the Father of Hassan, and sensible people tried to kill it before it killed them.

By the time Bo-Kah was a year old he fully understood such instructions as No, Lie down, Get off the bed, Come for a walk, Back home, and Naughty boy. He was so obviously harmless that Mrs. Haskell repented of her strictness and allowed him the occasional visit inside the house, bravely shutting her ears to the frightful din which he and Kushi made while chasing each other around the elegant dining table. Father and Bo-Kah adored each other. When it rained heavily father took him in and allowed him to sleep on his bed. Bo-Kah, for his part, regarded it as his castle and whenever reprimanded by anyone but father would jump on it as if to say, "Now you can't get me." The only thing he never quite accepted was the sight of father sitting motionless by his desk. Bo-Kah would anxiously eye him from his crouch on the bed, then clamber down and start licking his ankles and eventually biting them to see whether there was still life in the inert figure. When told off he would let himself out of the room and wait by the locked front door, indicating that he was bored and would someone please let him return to his den in the hollow of the olive tree.

Bo-Kah's fame spread far and wide and visitors from all over the country came to gaze at him. One afternoon an opulent-looking Arab couple stopped to look at the olive tree den before going into the house to knock at the door on the first floor. The man wore a dark suit and a *tarboosh*, a red cap with a black tassel, while the woman had on a shapeless black silk dress with a veil. The man looked distressed.

"*Ya mualem*, Learned Sir," he began without any of the usual oriental preambles, "the lady here has a request to make."

His wife lifted her black veil and I could see the pretty young face ravaged with weeping. "It's our little boy," she whispered. "He's got a growth on his groin. Our own doctors haven't been able to help him. Even your famous Dr. Yaffe doesn't know what to do about it."

Father was puzzled. "I'm a teacher, madam," he said, "not a physician."

"But you have a *debba*," the woman said pleadingly. "Our Wise Man says that if we apply a lotion made up of hyena excreta and vinegar, the growth will clear up. Please, *ya mualem*, may I collect your *debba's* leavings? It's for my son."

They were prevailed upon to accept a cup of Turkish coffee while I went down to the yard to search for the prescribed medicine.

"Will it help?" I asked after they had gone.

"Who knows? Poor little boy."

The next request for Bo-Kah's healing excreta came from an Arab peasant woman. She explained in her uncouth voice that her daughter was afflicted with jaundice. The doctors did not know how to treat it, but the Wise Man told her to collect hyena leavings and roast them on an open fire until they burned. "He promised the smell would cure the girl just like that." She snapped her middle finger against her thumb.

"You are welcome to collect as much as you like," father said. "My daughter will show you to his favorite spot."

To my surprise the woman made no attempt to follow me.

"The Wise Man said only a *debba's* leavings will cure my daughter," she said suspiciously. "Is that creature really a *debba*?"

"Of course it is."

"I've never heard of a *debba* chained like a city dog."

"*Allah* is my witness that Bo-Kah is a real *debba*," father solemnly pronounced.

The third and last of our patients was Jewish, an overblown oriental beauty who obstinately refused to reveal what she wanted the stuff for. After she had collected her fill father said she was probably going to brew it for a love potion.

One afternoon Bo-Kah disappeared. He had struggled free of his collar, eaten half of it for good measure, then slipped out through a hole in the fence which he had seen Kushi use as a getaway. That night father left all gates and doors open and paced up and down his room waiting for the return of the prodigal. At about midnight Bo-Kah stole in, made straight for father's room, and started bleating and licking his ankles. We concluded that he had gone out mating, for we had seen him trying to mount Kushi when she was on heat. He was given a new collar inscribed with his name, but a few days later he demonstrated in our presence how clever he was at wriggling free of it. Father would not hear of restricting him in a cage and said that Bo-Kah should be allowed to take his freedom whenever he felt the urge.

The following year father ran a summer camp on Mount Carmel and had Bo-Kah installed in a wooden kennel in a

remote corner of the site. It immediately became the camp-
ers' favorite haunt. Boys and girls between nine and fifteen
vied with one another for the honor of being the hyena's
appointed feeders and called on him every hour of the day
with offerings of meat and fruit. He put up with them
good-humoredly and when he had had enough he slowly
retreated inside his kennel and became invisible.

It was mating time again, or perhaps it was just the call of
the wild, for one morning when his feeders came to give
him fresh water, Bo-Kah was gone. When several days
passed with no news of him, gloom descended on the
camp. Father's face was set and I, who had never been
taught to pray, asked God every night in the darkness of
the tent to return Bo-Kah to us. One evening, just as we
were about to sit down to our meal, the familiar bleat was
heard from the direction of the kennel; Bo-Kah had come
back. Pandemonium broke out. Children and supervisors
stampeded to the far end of the camp to greet him, were
shocked to see how thin he had become, flew to the kitchen
tent, and came out laden with meat, fruit, bread, and jam,
whatever we could lay our hands on. Bo-Kah demolished
everything that was put before him and then settled to a
deep sleep from which he awoke only twenty-four hours
later.

He had been with us for nearly two years when he went
off again, having loosened a link in his chain without
taking off his collar. This time we were less anxious, trusting him to return home when he had had enough of independence. We later learned that while climbing a hillside
he saw a flock of sheep and stopped to look at them. The
Arab shepherd tried to drive him away with stones but
Bo-Kah, who had never been harmed by humans and had
no reason to fear them, stood his ground and bleated ami-
ably. The terrified shepherd abandoned his flock and ran
away shrieking *"Abu Hassan! Abu Hassan!"* until he
bumped into the village policeman and gasped out that a

demon hyena was killing his sheep and laughing among the corpses. The two men stalked back to see Bo-Kah walking slowly up the hill, still bleating for company. The policeman shot him dead. Only when they came out of their hiding to take a closer look did they notice the collar. It was all we got back.

12

Buy Hebrew

IN 1931 HAIFA WAS already a sizable town with a population of 50,000, of whom 16,000 were Jewish. It had become one of Palestine's three main cities; but while Jerusalem was the capital and as such above inter-urban rivalries, Tel Aviv and Haifa tried to surpass each other in civic enterprise. No sooner had Tel Aviv organized a carnival procession to celebrate the festival of Purim than Haifa launched an agricultural pageant to mark the feast of Shavuot. No sooner had Tel Aviv invented for carnival the mongrel word *adleyada*, than Haifa revived for Shavuot the old name Festival of the First Fruits.

The inspiration for the pageant came from ancient times, when the Children of Israel celebrated Shavuot by making the prescribed pilgrimage to Jerusalem and offering the first fruits of the land to the temple priesthood. Since there had been no temple in Eretz Israel for nearly two thousand years, it was authoritatively suggested that the ritual could be secularized and the tradition translated into modern idiom. Haifa, with its outlying agricultural settlements north and south, proclaimed itself an ideal setting for the revival.

The first pageants were modest and homely but the 1933 festival was planned on a more ambitious scale. It was based on a Talmudic eyewitness account of the ritual in the first century of the Common Era, when Agrippa I was King of Judea by the grace of Rome. Pilgrims who lived near

Jerusalem, the account said, took along fresh figs and grapes; those who had come from afar took dried figs and raisins. When they came within sight of the Holy City they stopped to arrange their first fruits in pretty baskets while messengers ran ahead to herald their approach. As each village formed itself into a group, the reedpipes struck up and the procession began moving, led by an ox wearing a garland of olive branches over its gilded horns. At the city gates the celebrants were received by the local artisans who greeted each group with the same formula: "Brethren, men of such and such a place, you are welcome."

Suddenly everybody around me was talking fruit trees, reedpipes, and oxen. Housewives were exhorted to donate their first jams and pickles of the season to a special home produce stall; schoolchildren wove baskets for the offerings and embroidered pretty things for the joint schools stall. A slope of Mount Carmel was taken over as the starting point of the pageant, and the ceremony was to reach its climax on the stage of the vast municipal amphitheater below Herzl Street.

A day or two before Shavuot, celebrants and their livestock began arriving from distant settlements and camped at the foot of a hill outside town. On the day, as a trumpet blast signaled the start of the proceedings, they climbed the hill from the back and began their spectacular descent into the center of town. There were mule-drawn carts magnificently arrayed with fruit, vegetables, and flowers, floats with poultry and dairy produce, herds of newborn calves, flocks of lambs, bands of reedpipes and tambourines. Pretty kibbutz girls in semi-oriental peasant costumes held ewe lambs in their arms, kibbutz men dressed as Arab shepherds led the flocks, groups of artisans—blacksmiths, carpenters, cobblers—marched in step, proudly displaying the tools of their trade. A posse of wild horsemen from Zichron Yaakov lent dash, while hundreds and hundreds of schoolchildren clad in white and crowned with myrtle joined the procession at pre-arranged points along the route and recited the traditional greeting:

"Brethren, men of Ziochron Yaakov, you are welcome."
"Brethren, men of Nahalal, you are welcome."
"Brethren, men of En Harod, you are welcome."

Haifa vibrated with bucolic sounds. Cattle lowed, sheep bleated, horses neighed, reedpipes squeaked; and above the hubbub and the cheering of the crowds rose the out-of-tune voices of excited schoolchildren singing over and over again a newly composed song which has since become the Shavuot anthem:

> *Baskets on our shoulders,*
> *Garlands on our heads,*
> *From far and wide we have come*
> *With the first fruits of the land*
> *From Judea and Samaria,*
> *From Jezreel and Galilee.*
> *Make way for us*
> *Bearers of the first fruits;*
> *Beat the drums*
> *And sound the pipes.*

It was a hot afternoon. By the time my group reached the packed amphitheater my myrtle crown had wilted and my white frock had lost its crispness. I sneaked out to take another look at the ewe lambs and the calves. I was not bothered by Hadar Hacarmel's shopping center's looking and smelling like a farmyard and was later surprised to hear people say that a modern city was hardly the right setting for rustic activities. I thought it had been a splendid day.

One of the objects of the Shavuot pageant, I knew, was to demonstrate the superior quality of Jewish farm produce. The great competitors were the Arab *fellaheen* who rode their donkeys into the middle of Hadar Hacarmel and offered housewives cheaper vegetables and fruit on their very doorstep. Russian-speaking Abdallah and his donkey did brisk business in my street and I was often sent downstairs to buy a *rotel* of green grapes or eggplants from him. The only legitimate way to stop housewives from buying Arab produce was to persuade them that it was inferior.

One particular exhortation to this effect was projected twice nightly on the screen of the amphitheater cinema before the beginning of the main feature film. It began with a close-up of a grocer's scales with two brass pans. When a disembodied hand dropped a small mucky egg into the pan on the right, it duly went down sending the empty one up; but when the same disembodied hand dropped a splendid-looking large egg into the empty left pan, it came down easily, sending the lighter one up. The message was clear enough and in case it was not the sub-titles spelled it out. The inferior egg was Arab, the superior one was a product of modern Jewish hen houses. Conclusion: Buy Best or, as the phrase then went, Buy Hebrew.

I was a regular cinema-goer in those days, being much taken with the lighthearted German film comedies which starred Willi Fritsch and pretty Lillian Harvey. Every Saturday evening, as I waited for the egg advertisement to make way for the feature film, I wondered why people needed so much reminding of the obvious, when everybody knew that Arab produce was inferior all along the line: Arab chickens were scrawny, Arab cows yielded thin milk, Arab fruits and vegetables were blighted. True enough, Arab produce was considerably cheaper, but at school and girl guides I had been inculcated with the doctrine that the saving of a few piasters did not justify what amounted to a betrayal of the national economy. Agriculture was the *yishuv's* lifeline. Greengrocers who stocked Arab produce were unpatriotic, and housewives who bought it ought to be ashamed of themselves for caring more for their pockets than for the needs of the nation. I had the greatest admiration for a young man nicknamed Trotsky who was said to have poured paraffin over a consignment of bananas delivered by an Arab grower to a Jewish greengrocer. Trotsky was a True Patriot.

The campaign was directed, however, not only against local Arab farm produce but against imported goods as well. Local Jewish industry was in its infancy and consumer goods were often below standard. Shoes came apart, colored fabrics ran, textiles shrank in the wash, jumpers lost their shape, pencil leads broke in the middle of sharpening. The words *totzeret ha'aretz,* made in Eretz Israel, became synonymous with inferior goods. Distributors were reluctant to market them and shopkeepers in the three main cities displayed shoes made in Czechoslovakia and Syria, textiles made in Britain, colored pencils made in Germany, toys made in Japan. Local manufacturers were finding it hard to win orders and many had to reduce their staff or shut down altogether.

It was characteristic of the times that the man who did most to further the cause of Jewish industry in Palestine was not a manufacturer anxious to save his business but a factory hand who had been laid off. His own line was shoemaking. Having made it clear from the outset that his quarrel was not with employers but with distributors and consumers, he called for a unified action. In December 1930, when unemployment in the footwear trade was rising and most people were unconcernedly buying imported shoes, he organized a cobblers' march through the streets of Tel Aviv.

The human composition of the march was probably unique in the annals of industrial disputes; out-of-work employees marched shoulder to shoulder with frustrated employers, protesting with one voice against hard-hearted shopkeepers and consumers. In their eagerness to call attention to their grievance the marchers had neglected to seek permission for the demonstration, and before they were halfway down Allenby Street the Tel Aviv police came down on them. There were ugly clashes and several arrests. The cause of *totzeret ha'haretz* could claim its first martyrs.

The organizer of the cobblers' march was in his late twenties at the time. His original name was Moshe Nudelman; on his arrival in Palestine from his native Russia he changed it to Moshe Halutz, *halutz* meaning pioneer; when I came to hear of him he was already known by the nickname Trotsky which he had earned not only because of his uncanny physical resemblance to the Soviet revolutionary but also because of his own anarchic methods.

The stories about him were legion. Once he distributed leaflets calling on customers to take their custom away from a well-known Tel Aviv shop which was displaying imported footwear. When his call went unheeded he quixotically barred the entrance to the shop with his body. On another occasion he organized picket lines outside several offending shoe shops and actually succeeded in bringing business to a standstill. When the enraged shopkeepers came out to protest he had their shop windows smashed. One day he was introduced to a young man who had taken it into his head to pioneer a Hebrew film industry and was seeking a way to persuade reluctant cinema owners to screen his own primitively produced Hebrew newsreel.

"First you must talk to them," Trotsky said reasonably.

"I have."

"And?"

"They say British Gaumont is better."

"They do, do they? That settles it. Unemployed cobblers will be smuggled into every film theater in town and when British Gaumont comes on they will fling black ink on the screen."

Trotsky's assistance was declined. He went back to picketing shoe shops and smashing shop windows. He was often beaten and arrested. Every time he came out of prison he vowed he would not give up until the local footwear industry won the day. "In Russia I was arrested for championing the cause of the Hebrew people," he wrote after he had served his thirty-fifth prison sentence. "In the Land of Israel I am being arrested for championing the cause of the Hebrew shoe."

As time went by, the range of his zeal widened to include the building industry which was having a boom thanks to the well-to-do German immigrants of the early thirties. Most contractors ordered their supplies of cement from Nesher, a factory near Haifa which I had been taken to visit as part of my school curriculum. Some contractors, however, preferred imported cement. When word reached Trotsky that a consignment of foreign cement had just been unloaded in Jaffa and put in storage, he stole in during the night and turned the water hoses on. By morning several hundred sacks of cement had hardened into blocks. The distraught contractor appealed to Nesher for an urgent replacement and, having learned his lesson, cancelled all future orders from abroad. Trotsky showed no fear or favor. When he learned that Dr. Hayim Weizmann, then head of the World Zionist Organization, had had some slabs of Italian marble imported for his new house at Rehovot, he wrote him a severe letter of reprimand.

Trotsky had the dedication of a prophet. In between exploits which fired the imagination of the young and gave publicity to his campaign, he held meetings with distributors, called on importers and appealed to the leaders of the *yishuv* to support his efforts. It was due to his incessant badgering that the Society for the Promotion of Eretz Israel-Made Consumer Goods was eventually set up, with himself as chairman. Public recognition brought respectability; sabotage was abandoned and moral pressure was introduced instead.

Some time in 1933 the Society organized a nationwide *Totzeret Ha'aretz* Week. My duty, as a patriotic girl guide and a firm believer in Buy Hebrew, was to go from door to door to persuade housewives not to buy any foreign-made goods that week.

My list was full of such names as Freudenthal, Grünwald, Bartfeld, and Königsberger, all recent arrivals from Germany. My friend Zephyra and I knocked at the first door on our list.

"Shalom," we said simultaneously.

"Shalom shalom. *Was wünschen Sie?*"

"We would be grateful if you would kindly give an undertaking to buy only locally made goods all this week," I recited in Hebrew.

"*Bitte?*"

Zephyra repeated the message in a less formal style.

"*Ich verstehe nicht.*" The door closed.

When our second and third attempt met with the same uncomprehending reaction, Zephyra and I had my mother make up for us a short speech in German which we learned parrot fashion until we felt we were word perfect. We then went back to our beat.

"*Guten Abend,*" I said in what I thought was an impeccable German accent. "We are calling on behalf of *totzeret ha'aretz*. This week is *Totzeret Ha'aretz* Week. We have come to ask you to undertake to buy only *totzeret ha'aretz* all this week and to sign your name on this sheet to show that you agree." The sheet had two columns, one with a list of addresses we were to call on, the other with signatures already collected. The woman on the doorstep looked stone-faced.

"*Totzeret ha'aretz* is no good."

"If you support it, it will improve."

"Has any of the neighbors signed?"

"Oh, yes. Look, the list says Mrs. Sachs, Dr. and Frau Levy, Mrs. Hauser."

The woman picked up the sheet and examined it with reluctance. Some of the signatures had been written in German, some in a large, painstaking Hebrew scrawl.

"Are you two going to come back to check whether I've kept my word?"

"Oh, no, it's entirely voluntary."

"What's there to make me keep it?" the woman asked suspiciously.

We were prepared for just such a question. "It's a moral obligation," Zephyra said in German with a winning smile. The woman signed without further ado. "Buy Hebrew," we called over our shoulder by way of good-bye.

The companion slogan of Buy Hebrew was Hebrew Labor. Attempts to introduce Hebrew labor into the most menial of employments had started well before the turn of the century, but Jewish farmers, and later Jewish building contractors, often preferred Arabs. It was a matter of hard economics. Hebrew laborers were members of a trade union and had to be paid an agreed wage; Arab laborers accepted less and had never heard of industrial action. To make matters worse for Jewish workmen hundreds of destitute Arabs from the Hauran region of Trans-Jordan crossed into Palestine and hired themselves out by the day at very low wages. It made little difference that they were unskilled and backward and that Haurani workmanship had come to mean cheap and shoddy workmanship; developers still had use for them.

One afternoon word went around that a gang of Hauranis was unloading sacks of cement at a certain building site. The Jewish contractor was nowhere within sight. While some of us stood around chanting "Hebrew Labor," a rival gang came running, pushed the uncomprehending Hauranis out of the way, and took over. The new arrivals did not look to me like laborers. Two of them had ties on and one sported a dark blue suit of the kind that only dandies were known to wear.

"It's not the money we're after," the dandy explained to the gathered crowd. "It's the principle of the thing. Hebrew Labor is the lifeline of the country." Like the legendary Trotsky, the dandy was a True Patriot.

Other True Patriots made it their business to promote the Hebrew language or, as they put it, to defend it. The enemies from whom they sought to defend it were the new immigrants who clung to their native tongues and spoke them in offices, shops, cafés, and buses. "Hebrews, speak Hebrew," ran the Defenders' slogan. I gave them my unquestioning support until I passed by an open-air meeting of theirs and overheard such non-Hebrew words as *idéal, democratia* and *re-organizatsia*. My mother was amused when I indignantly reported that the Defenders were hypocrites.

"They are not hypocrites. There simply aren't any Hebrew equivalents for these words."

"What about immigrants who speak German or Polish or whatever? The Defenders say people should not offer them employment until they have learned to speak Hebrew properly."

Mother was no longer amused. "Nobody should be penalized for being a slow learner," she said. "Everyone should be allowed to learn at his own pace."

13

Music Ho!

WHEN WE WERE STILL LIVING at Bat Galim my mother had a framed portrait hanging on her bedroom wall, showing a man with slightly wavy auburn hair, sideburns and a prominent nose.

"Who is it?" I asked.

"He's a famous composer."

"What does a composer do?"

Mother explained.

"What's his name?"

"Chopin."

Mother went on to say that when she was a young girl in Warsaw she had played some of his music and that one day I too might be able to do so. I did not give the matter a thought for several years, until we moved to Shapira's House at Hadar Hacarmel.

I was lying in bed one night when through the open window the sound of piano playing wafted in. It was beautiful. I learned that the music was played by Mr. Shapira's eldest daughter who was training to be a professional pianist and practiced every night. The sounds kept floating from the open windows of the third floor into my own little room on the ground floor, filling it with a kind of enchantment I had never experienced before. Night after night I lay in bed trying not to fall asleep so as not to miss any of the beautiful music, and morning after morning I woke up annoyed with myself for having dropped off before the music had stopped.

"Can I learn to play the piano?" I asked one morning over breakfast. A child's breakfast started with a spoonful of cod-liver oil, the vilest tasting medication ever invented by man.

"Get your cod-liver oil down first," I was told.

"Can I learn to play the piano?" I repeated a moment later.

"When you are eight," I was promised. Eight was considered the proper age for starting music lessons at the Haifa Institute of Music. I was only six.

When the great day at long last came my mother shook her head.

"We cannot afford to buy a piano. It will have to be a violin. Mr. Klein will lend you one for a start."

And so, frustrated but curious nonetheless, I began taking violin lessons on a borrowed quarter-size instrument. I bowed, and pressed, and put up with the discomfort on my left shoulder, and asked questions which Mr. Klein said were intelligent, but the music did not come. After a month or two my father took me to Kowalsky's Music Store to buy me a record.

On the way to the store my father told me something of Mr. Kowalsky's life story. As a child he studied music with a well-known cantor in his native Russia and became a synagogue choirboy. Armed with this expertise he immigrated to Palestine to become a pioneer and joined a group of settlers near the Jordan. Overnight the choirboy became a man of muscle. He plowed, kept watch, drove off marauding Bedouins, and slept out-of-doors on a pile of straw. One night, my father went on, Kowalsky woke up to a suspicious rustle. Hand on trigger, he noiselessly searched the dark for an invisible enemy but encountered nobody. Hardly had he settled back onto his pile of straw when he heard the rustle again, this time right by his side.

It was a snake. Seizing it by the head with one hand he shot it dead with the other. A few years later he moved to Jerusalem and started teaching music at the Mission schools, at the same time forming a professional brass band. During the war he was appointed conductor of the Ottoman Military Band and afterwards he opened two music stores, one in Jerusalem and one in Haifa.

The Haifa branch was situated on the ground floor of an Arab house in the Old City; large, dark, a real Aladdin's cave. Father explained that he was looking for some inspiring violin music for his little daughter and the assistant put on a Romanian *doina* to see if I liked it. I had never heard a violin played by anyone other than myself and expected the record to yield the same tormented, screechy, off-pitch sounds I was so familiar with. When it did not, I wondered where the violin had got to. Seeing that I was not much taken with the violin record, father bought me two vocal ones as well.

There was no proper gramophone at home, but Mrs. Haskell had given me an American-made toy one, together with a small record which introduced me to "Yankee Doodle Went to Town." It had a handle shaped like a sardine tin opener with a tendency to revolve back at great speed and flatten the spring down in less than a minute; but when it was in a working mood it was powerful enough to cope with a full-size 78, requiring finger spinning only for the last few grooves. That was how I first heard Caruso sing Cavaradossi's farewell aria, "E lucevan le stelle," from the third act of Puccini's *Tosca*. It was a single-sided record and for a long time I believed that the assistant at Kowalsky's had cheated us. My second vocal record was more satisfying. It was double-sided, with a soprano singing the Bell Song from Léo Delibes's *Lakmé* on the one side, and one of Rachel's arias from Halévy's *La Juive* on the other. I played all three so often that I was eventually able to squeak some phrases—tenor and soprano freely transposed to suit a child's range—with a measure of accuracy though without the words. When I informed my father that singing was more fun than fiddling he surprised me by saying that had he not been a biologist he would have liked to be an opera singer. My violin lessons were allowed to lapse.

A year or so later I began to take piano lessons at the Haifa Institute of Music, first practicing daily on a neighbor's piano and later on a second-hand black upright purchased after many calculations and much trepidation. Mother had paid for it twenty-five Palestinian pounds, the equivalent of two months' earnings.

It was the practice of the Institute to hold public examinations at the end of each academic year, with a crowd of doting parents and not-so-doting friends keenly listening to examinees performing on their chosen instruments. Although I had been taking lessons for only four weeks before examination date, I was not exempt from the ordeal. My piano teacher introduced me to the audience as a "promising pupil" who in four weeks had made remarkable progress, and pushed me onto the platform. The stuffy hall was full of eyes and the acrid smell of sweat; when I finished playing my two little pieces on the grand piano the audience politely clapped and I did not know what to do next. In the following years I saw the same scene reenacted time and again. There was always a "promising pupil" who had made "remarkable progress" in a comparatively short time and there was always a proud and hopeful teacher to acknowledge the applause generously given to a little newcomer glued with embarrassment to the raised piano stool.

The foundress and directress of the Institute, a sister of Dr. Hayim Weizmann's, wanted us to acquire an all-round musical education and insisted that pupils of all grades and instruments should attend theory classes as well. I could see no connection between the sterile exercises we were made to do and the beauty that was music, but one afternoon the theory teacher partly redeemed himself when he mentioned a "musical pioneer" whose work we were urged to seek out. That musical pioneer was Mordechai Golinkin, founder and conductor of the Palestine Opera.

Golinkin was born in the Ukraine in 1875 and had his first musical training from the same cantor who had taught snake killer music seller Kowalsky. Golinkin too had more strength in his fists than a choirboy was expected to have and demonstrated it successfully to some rowdies who had tried to bait him for his Jewishness. After graduating from the Warsaw Conservatoire he returned to Russia and by 1918 was the resident conductor of the Maryinsky Opera Theater in St. Petersburg. At the height of his career he decided to go into the musical wilderness that was Palestine to start a Hebrew opera company.

He was a practical dreamer. First he published a brochure in Russian promoting his project and in 1920 he conducted a fund-raising concert with Chaliapin participating. Three years later he was ready. At the beginning of 1923—when my parents were converting sand dunes into a suburb called Bat Galim—he sailed to Palestine with a bagful of operatic libretti translated into Hebrew by the best literary talents of the day. On July 24 of that year he put on the first ever performance in Hebrew of Verdi's *La Traviata* at the Eden Film Theater in Tel Aviv.

It was a gala occasion. The imagination of every culture-loving resident had been fired by Golinkin's single-mindedness and Tel Aviv's *crème de la crème*, headed by Mayor Meir Diezengoff, had accepted the invitation to attend. Palestinian audiences, however, were not used to punctuality. Public performances, like inter-urban buses, started well past the advertised time in order to give ample chance to stragglers, undecided passersby, and the ever-hopefuls. Golinkin was new to the ways of the country and a firm follower of the Maryinsky tradition of artistic discipline. When at the advertized hour the hall was still half empty, he ordered the incredulous ushers to lock the doors and raised his baton. Latecomers, including His Worship the Mayor, were made to wait outside until the end of the first act.

La Traviata was followed by an ambitious repertoire including *Aida*, *Tosca*, *Samson and Delilah*, and *La Juive*, all sung in Hebrew by local talent as well as guest artists. The difficulties were enormous. When Golinkin left for the States the Palestine Opera petered out, to be revived only on his return in the early thirties. When I first heard of him Golinkin was about to launch the 1933 opera season with a gala performance of Verdi's *Rigoletto* in the presence of no less exalted a personage than the Empress of Abyssinia.

Empress Waizero Manin, wife of Haile Selassie, King of Kings and Lion of Judah, was on a world tour, escorted by her Foreign Minister, the court physician, a princess, a prince or two, and several other imperial dignitaries. Her progress through Palestine was followed with curiosity. She had spent the morning of October 8 with the Abyssinian community in Jerusalem and was then driven to Tel Aviv and put up at the flag-bedecked Palatine Hotel, the most modern and luxurious in town. In the evening a banquet was given in her honor by Mayor Diezengoff, after which he was to escort her to the opera.

Golinkin had insisted that all posters and announcements advertising *Rigoletto* should carry a warning that the performance would begin at 8:30 p.m. sharp. He had rehearsed the Abyssinian anthem with the orchestra and had personally supervised the hanging of the Abyssinian, British, and Jewish flags in the hall. By 8:30 all seats had been taken up except the seats of honor. There was no question of locking the imperial party out and risking an international diplomatic scandal. Golinkin held up the performance. After some delay a message came through to the effect that Her Imperial Majesty had not yet finished dinner.

Three-quarters of an hour past the scheduled time Empress, imperial party, and an unflappable Mayor entered the auditorium and acknowledged the audience who had respectfully risen to their feet. After the playing of the British and Abyssinian national anthems as well as *Hatikva*, and the inevitable shuffling and throat clearing, everybody settled down for the main business of the evening. When the performance ended it was past one o'clock in the morning. *Ha'aretz* later reported that the Empress and her entourage had followed the opera with great interest and sat through to the very end.

The morning after the performance an equerry called on soprano Rap-Janowska and commanded her to accompany him to the imperial suite at the Palatine Hotel to await the Empress's pleasure. There was a long anxious wait in the antechamber which ended with a bleary-eyed Imperial Majesty coming out of her bedroom to tell the singing-woman that she had been well pleased with her rendering of Gilda. The Empress then beckoned to her Foreign Minister to fetch her jewel box, selected a gold bracelet, and clasped it around the singer's wrist. She also gave Mrs. Rap-Janowska a gold medallion with the Emperor's likeness to wear around her neck and invited her to perform at the Abyssinian court. The invitation was never taken up. Instead, the Empress returned to Palestine in May 1936, fleeing with Emperor Haile Selassie from Italian aggression and finding temporary refuge in Jerusalem.

Some time after *Rigoletto* the Palestine Opera came to Haifa to give a matinee of Rossini's *The Barber of Seville* at a cinema which only a few years earlier had seemed the last word in modernity but now looked primitive and shabby. I did not quite know what to expect and was overwhelmed by what I saw. Plot, decor, period, operatic conventions—all were strange, all were fascinating. The singing was a different matter. Like most natives of my age my musical expectations were based on what little singing I had heard on record, and since the only soprano I had heard on record was Amelita Galli-Curci, I expected all sopranos to sound just like her. The Palestine Opera soprano, however deserving, was no Galli-Curci; her Rosina was shrill and her high notes as piercing as a boy scout's whistle. Some of my schoolmates, recently arrived from Germany and no strangers to opera, sniggered and whispered that the singing was a regular caterwauling.

Even so, I continued to attend every schools' matinee by the Palestine Opera and a new rival company which, between them, introduced me to a repertoire ranging from Lehár's *The Merry Widow* to Puccini's *Madame Butterfly*. The quality of the singing varied, but I never saw a single vacant seat.

14

The Great Years

OF ALL RECREATIONS available to me during term time,
bathing in the sea was the most agreeable. As far as parents were concerned the swimming season opened on
June 1, but when I argued that bathing should be regu-
lated by temperature rather than calendar, I was allowed
in the water during a freak heat wave in the middle of
February.

Apart from my native Bat Galim, which was too far from
Hadar Hacarmel for an afternoon jaunt, Haifa's only beach
was the one by the German Colony. The quickest way to
reach it on foot was through the Arab Old City, a maze of
narrow alleyways and courtyards, with fat women
balancing baskets on their heads, donkeys pushing
pedestrians into the gutter, and bottom-pinching youths
lurking in doorways. I was walking fast with my towel and
bathing costume rolled under my arm when a little girl,
four or five at the most, came out of a courtyard and hissed:
"I spit on you, *yahudim*."

The spit caught me on the left ankle, but I knew that
bending down would invite further abuse, as would
breaking into a run. When I got to the beach I scrubbed the
insult off with sand and sea water.

The German Colony beach was an enclosed area in the
curve of the bay, much favored by mothers with young
children. Bathers had to pay to get in and were expected to
change in ill-smelling wooden huts. Sometimes I took

along a picnic basket and swapped contents with other children similarly provided. If I had half a piaster to spare I disregarded friendly advice about health hazards and bought from one of the strolling Arab vendors an unwrapped water ice on a stick called *booza*. The sea was nearly always calm.

Then the beach began to shrink. Gangs of laborers pushed bathers out of the way, dropped huge blocks of concrete into the water and installed an outlandish giant machine which went by the hitherto unknown name of crane. The sea too was shrinking. The water was getting shallower, part of the swimming area was fenced off, and one afternoon I was told that within a week the beach would be out of bounds. When I came down all the same I was staggered. The sea had receded beyond reach. The spot where I used to swim had been filled in with gravel and pitch, and a steam roller was flattening it. When I next passed by there was nothing left of the beach and what used to be a sea was now a smooth asphalt stretch called Kings Road (later Independence Road).

It was a nuisance, but at the same time it was exciting, for it meant that work was going apace to transform Haifa's primitive landing place into one of the most modern ports along the Mediterranean. At school I learned that the British government had ordered the first soundings as early as 1920 and that Parliament had authorized a loan to finance the project. The main breakwater was begun in October 1929, shortly after the Arab disturbances. Four years later the port of Haifa was completed as we know it today.

The inauguration ceremony was fixed for Tuesday, October 31, 1933, and was to be held in the presence of a thousand dignitaries from the Jewish and Arab communities. The preceding weeks, however, the Arab leadership had been protesting against Jewish immigration, and on the Friday before October 31 things came to a head. There were inflammatory speeches in the mosques, unauthorized demonstrations, attempts on Jewish lives, clashes with the British security forces, and casualties on all sides. The Arabs called a general strike. To avoid any possible violence during the inauguration ceremony all invitations were cancelled at the last moment and only government officials and a handful of reporters were allowed to attend.

October 31 was one of those mild autumn days which felt uncomfortably warm because summer clothes had already been put away in mothballs and everybody was in woolens. In spite of the Arab strike Haifa looked festive. Public buildings and shipping offices flew flags while thousands of Haifaites crowded on rooftops and balconies overlooking the harbor to watch the proceedings through old army binoculars and dainty opera glasses. Visibility was perfect.

From my own rooftop perch the harbor did not look as virginal as I had imagined it would on inauguration day. The night before, the Royal navy patrol sloop *Hastings* had quietly slipped in, and a launch was lying by with steam up. The High Commissioner, Sir Arthur Grenfell Wauchope, who had flown over from Jerusalem earlier that morning, was already on board and at precisely 11:20 he and his party embarked on the launch. They were sailing out to board the British liner *Lancastrian Prince*, which had arrived the day before and had anchored in the open sea. At 11:35—the British preoccupation with precision seemed bizarre to us natives—the *Lancastrian Prince* weighed anchor and escorted by Royal Air Force planes flying in formation sailed majestically into harbor. Just as she crossed the entrance a seven-gun salute was fired, followed by a seventeen-gun salute from the *Hastings*. At 12:15 the first liner to enter the new port of Haifa had docked. When the High Commissioner stepped down the British national anthem was played.

The rest of the ceremony was concealed from view and information was later gleaned from the scanty reports in the press. The British guests of honor had taken their seats on a platform bedecked with flags and flowers as planned, but instead of a festive gathering of local dignitaries they faced rows and rows of empty wooden chairs; the press estimated the number of government officials present at eighty at the most. The High Commissioner made his prepared speech all the same and so did the guests of honor; contrary to accepted procedure the speeches were not translated into either Arabic or Hebrew. There followed a lunch on board the *Lancastrian Prince* with bagpipe music provided by the band of the 2nd Battalion of the Seaforth Highlanders. The BBC had a commentator describing the proceedings to listeners in Great Britain and at 1:30—that precision again—the Colonial Secretary came up on the radio telegraph line from London and offered his congratulations to the High Commissioner and the people of Palestine.

That same year I was taken to the harbor to meet my sister who had completed her modern ballet training in Vienna and Dresden and was due back on one of the Italian Lloyd Triestino twin ships which operated between Trieste and Haifa. When she first sailed out some three years earlier, I had kissed her good-bye on the water's edge and watched her being taken to the distant ship by rowing boat. Now she ran lightly down the gangway and threw her arms around my mother and me within touching distance of the *Adria*. It was nothing short of a miracle.

While the port was under construction it was still possible to see sand-colored single-humped camels aloofly trotting along Haifa's side streets, but when I was told of a blue and white camel flying over the roofs of Tel Aviv I thought it was sheer oriental fantasy. It turned out to be an artist's fantasy; the Flying Camel had just been adopted as the emblem of an international trade fair which was to be held in Tel Aviv in the spring of 1932, the first of the three great Levant Fairs of the thirties.

There were two versions concerning the origin of the Flying Camel. According to one, the Jewish Board of Commerce and Industry who had initiated the fair, had asked Tel Aviv's Town Architect to suggest an emblem which would symbolize its potential impact on the entire East. When he came up with a sketch of a traditional caravan led by a rider on a donkey, the board members turned up their noses.

"Camels are not a bad idea for a Levant Fair, but these camels won't do. They look lethargic."

The architect produced another sketch showing camels in a slightly more animated trot.

"No, it isn't quite right."

The architect produced a sketch of a single camel in full gallop.

"No, it's still not quite right."

"What the hell do you want then?" The architect angrily snatched his sketches off the drawing board. "A flying camel?"

"That's a good idea. See what you can do."

According to the second version the emblem owed its derivation to a contemptuous remark made by the mayor of Jaffa. The Board had invited him to organize a pavilion which would exhibit Palestinian-made products.

"It will give a boost to local Arab industry," they assured him. "It's going to be the greatest trade fair ever held in the Levant."

"Not on your life it won't," the mayor scoffed. "There will no more be a Levant Fair in Tel Aviv than a camel will grow wings."

Sure enough the Levant Fair did come into being and

the camel did grow wings. There were Flying Camel posters, Flying Camel flags, Flying Camel badges. The 1932 fair drew 1,200 exhibitors from twenty-three countries and gave the hoped-for boost to exports and imports. No sooner was it over than preparations began for the next fair which was to be held on a gigantic scale. A virgin sand dune outside Tel Aviv was leveled and coated with asphalt; splendid wide roads were built and a permanent exhibition center began to grow, with attractive pavilions, entertainment grounds, a special telephone exchange and, miraculously, flower beds and patches of lawn. The official opening took place on April 26, 1934.

This time there were two thousand exhibitors from thirty-six countries. After the High Commissioner had declared the second Levant Fair open, the British national anthem and *Hatikva* were played. It was an unusually muggy day for April. Hardly had the distinguished guests slumped back into their seats when the band struck up the *Marseillaise*, then the Italian national anthem, then the Polish, the Syrian, the Algerian, the German, the Japanese, all thirty-six of them. There was nothing for it but to be up and standing in the heat for a full hour and a half.

For the next few days the press raved about the magnificence of the pavilions and the elegance, opulence, and modernity of the display. Part of the month-long Levant Fair coincided with the Passover school holidays. When I mentioned at home that some of my classmates were being allowed to go to the fair on their own, my mother replied as I had hoped she would: "You can go too if you like. You won't get lost I suppose."

It was arranged that I would stay with Aunt Helena who had moved from Rehovot to Tel Aviv. Mother took me to the main Haifa Railway Station in the Old City, put me in a third-class carriage, and shoved my half-fare ticket into my dress pocket.

"Would you mind looking after her?" she asked a sweaty

woman surrounded by parcels. "It's the first time she's gone by train on her own."

The third-class carriage was already full beyond capacity. There were boy scouts and girl guides with rucksacks, families with babies, Arab peasants with chickens in wire coops. Every wooden bench designed for two had three or four claimants fighting to get somebody off it. As soon as the train got moving the sweaty woman picked up her parcels and beckoned to me to follow her.

"I'm suffocating. Let's go somewhere else."

The other third-class carriages were equally overcrowded. The woman opened the door of a first-class compartment and I caught a glimpse of black leather upholstered benches with an immaculately white antimacassar on the back of each seat. Two opulent-looking Arabs in red *tarbooshes* looked up with displeasure and the woman hastily closed the door. She settled for an unoccupied second-class compartment with beautifully sprung seats covered with rush matting. When the inspector came around she handed him her ticket and mine without batting an eyelid.

"Pay extra," he said with severity. Like all inspectors, ticket sellers, train drivers, and porters on Palestine Railways, he was an Arab.

"No pay extra," the woman said in pidgin Arabic. "Third class no sit. No sit, I go second."

"You third class quick quick," the inspector shouted, falling too into pidgin Arabic in the common delusion that he would thus be better understood by a foreigner.

"Third class no sit. I pay money sit. No sit, I go second."

They argued thunderously for a little longer; then the inspector punched our tickets and closed the compartment door behind him. We were not disturbed any more.

At Lydda Junction my protectress disappeared and I was left to wait on my own for my connection to Tel Aviv-Jaffa. There was no timetable and no stationmaster, and the milling crowds had no more idea which train would go to Tel Aviv than I. When what appeared to be the right train at long last pulled in I was sucked in by the onrush and spewed into a compartment full of veiled Arab women and children. As I noticed later, it was one of those third-class compartments marked Ladies Only.

Once the train got going one of the women drew the blind over the door, lifted her veil, pulled out a breast, and began suckling her baby. She did not look much older than fifteen. There were four women in the compartment and about as many young children. It looked like a family party. The women, after they had lifted their veils, were all young and gay. They talked in shrill voices and offered the children and one another sunflower seeds which they cracked with great expertise, swallowing the soft center and spitting the shells under my feet.

There was a great deal of whispering and giggling. The most audacious of the four said pointing to my dark hair and face, "You are like us."

I did not know what the correct form was in a situation like this. All I knew was that on no account was I to coo over the little children and say how lovely they were, for fear of casting an evil eye on them. I said the first thing that came into my head: "Are you all sisters?"

There was a loud guffaw followed by a whispered consultation; then the audacious young woman offered me a paper cornet full of sunflower seeds.

"*Tfaddali*, have some."

While I was cracking and spitting out shells as best I could the women told me they were going to Jaffa to attend a relative's wedding. Their menfolk were sitting apart in another compartment. I said I was going to see my aunt in Tel Aviv.

"Are you spoken for?"

"No, I'm still at school."

"A big girl like you still at school?"

"I've got five more years to go."

The woman looked uncomprehending. I stood up against the door to demonstrate my small stature, indicated a point well above my head and said I would be wed the day I grew to be that tall.

"Next week?" they asked.

I had an inspiration. "How many sons have you got?" I asked the young mother who had been suckling her baby.

"This is my first. *Inshallah*, God willing, I shall bear my husband many more."

"I'll be wed the day you have five sons," I said, counting five on my fingers.

They were shocked. "It's not right to restrain a girl that long."

When I got off at Tel Aviv they crowded by the window, their black veils down again, waving good-bye. They had held up their hands to show five, five being not only the number of years I would have to wait for my wedding day but also a magic number which brought good luck to the believers.

I had no idea how to get to my aunt's place on Rothschild Boulevard and dusk was already giving way to night. With temerity born out of need I walked up to one of the two-horse *diligences* waiting at the station yard and gave the driver my aunt's address. As I was climbing in I heard him call out to his mates in Yiddish; all I could make out was the word for little girl. I had never known a *diligence* to be driven by a Jew and was relieved to be spared the intimidating ritual of arguing over the fare with a haggling Arab when my Aunt Helena, curious to see who had stopped outside her block of flats in such style, came out and saw me fumbling in my pocket.

"How much does he want?" she asked even before she hugged me.

I told her.

"Shame on you," she turned angrily on the driver,

"taking advantage of a simple little girl. Here, that's enough."

She pushed into his hand about half of what he had asked and he departed without protest. I later realized that the station was only a couple of minutes' walk from my aunt's.

The following morning I met a Haifa classmate at a pre-arranged rendezvous—only I was two hours late because I had lost my way—and we made for the exhibition grounds. The first thing we saw was the Flying Camel commanding the view from the top of a tall slim tower at the entrance. Once past the gates we did not know which way to look first. There were the magnificent national pavilions of such enticing countries as Italy, France, Switzerland, Bulgaria, Poland, Rumania, Czechoslovakia, and Sweden, with the British pavilion the largest of them all. There was a breathtaking International Pavilion and there were pavilions within pavilions for such countries as Syria, Hungary, Finland, and many others. The Palestine Pavilion displayed the country's achievements in agriculture and commerce while the *Totzeret Ha'aretz* Palace had a dazzling array of goods and foods only slightly marred by a smell of cheese. There were also bands, film theaters, ice cream parlors, and a fairground called Luna Park, the first ever to be seen in Palestine. When the month was over I read that the fair had attracted 600,000 visitors from all over the world, about twice the entire Jewish population of Palestine.

The 1934 Levant Fair was the second of its kind and, as it happened, also the last. By the time the third one opened in 1936, the Arab Revolt had broken out and the fair folded up within days, never to be revived. The Flying Camel, however, had contributed to the development of the country in another way.

Since the 1934 Levant Fair coincided with Tel Aviv's twenty-fifth anniversary and large numbers of tourists were expected, Mayor Diezengoff had conceived the pioneering idea of enabling them to arrive by air. A landing strip was prepared a few miles southeast of Tel Aviv and on April 26, the day the Levant Fair was opened, it was officially inaugurated by the High Commissioner who had flown in from a small military airfield near Jerusalem, only minutes away.

In the blaze of publicity surrounding the Levant Fair, the occasion would have passed virtually unnoticed had the High Commissioner not referred to it in his opening speech at the fair. "I feel I have begun the day well," Sir Arthur Grenfell Wauchope said, "by flying from Jerusalem to the new landing ground at Lydda, which I hope will be of some service to the Fair and in future to all Palestine."

That modest landing ground was the beginning of Lod (Lydda) International Airport. Among the first companies to launch a regular air service to Palestine were the Polish LOT and the Italian Ala Littoria. Aeroplanes were still rare enough for young people to rush out at the sound of a distant drone to watch them fly over the sea. I longed to fly with them.

15

A Taste of Adventure

EVEN BEFORE THE COMPLETION of the port Haifa and the introduction of an air service from Lydda, I had been dreaming of travel. My sister had returned from her years abroad with stories of adventures in Austria, Germany, and Switzerland; my brother was about to go to the States for his studies; I thought I might one day motorcycle to France and England.

The inspiration for such an ambition had come from a group of young athletes who had done just that. Tel Aviv had been preparing for its first international all-Jewish games, and since the building of an Olympic stadium required large sums of money, the *Maccabi* sports club decided to raise some by undertaking a sponsored motorcycle ride all the way to London. In May of 1931 twelve members mounted their motorbikes and rode out of Tel Aviv. Many had predicted that they would not get much further than Beer Sheba, but the young Maccabeans rode through the Sinai desert, Egypt, Greece, Yugoslavia, Austria, Germany, and France, put their machines on a channel ferry and on June 12 reached London. Their ride produced the desired response and quickened public interest in the games throughout Europe. Three days after their arrival the Lord Mayor of London sent them a letter to take back home, which read as follows:

The Lord Mayor Office
Guildhall, London E.C.2
15th June 1931

To
The Jewish Youth of Palestine:

I congratulate your Motor Cyclists, who have so successfully overcome the difficulties and dangers of the
long journey from Palestine to London and I sincerely
trust they will attain the object of this Expedition
namely the building of a Jewish Sports Stadium in
Palestine and the encouragement of athletics among
Jewish youth.

I am in entire sympathy with international athletics
movements, which do so much to encourage goodwill
and understanding among the people of different races
and for this reason I shall be glad to know in due time
that your efforts have been crowned with success.

Yours very sincerely
Sir William P. Neal
Lord Mayor

After that successful expedition going abroad by motorcycle became every daredevil's dream. Two of my sister's
friends had ridden their motorbikes to Greece and back. I
myself had already ridden pillion on a motorbike pur-
loined by an older classmate, and when we were both
thrown off with no bones broken I decided it was not such
a dangerous sport after all. I began to look forward to my
grand tour of Europe by motorcycle.

Until then however there were lots of places to be
explored in my own country. On the first day of each
month—by the Jewish lunar calendar—I went on a school
hike from which no one was exempt except on doctor's
orders. During the Passover holidays the school organized longer hikes which required much preparation.
Boots were examined for comfort, rucksacks for de-
pendability, blankets for weight. Every item on the
hiker's list was inspected well in advance and a marching
drill held with full packs on.

My father, the arch-hiker, led the more ambitious expeditions and took us along paths rarely trodden by
Jewish hikers. We climbed Mount Tabor and the Hill of
Moreh. We walked down Wadi Kelt on the way to the
Dead Sea and looked up at the inaccessible monastic cells
carved into the sheer rock. We swam in Lake Hula, since
drained and turned into arable land, and bathed in El
Hamma hot springs, then patronized solely by Arabs. Before entering an Arab village girls changed from shorts
into skirts and all were warned to close ranks. My father
would seek out the *moochtar*, the chosen chief, for an exchange of civilities and eventually ask permission to refill
our canteens from the village well. At night we slept on
the floors of Jewish schoolhouses curled up in our blankets, boys against one wall and girls against another.

One year a group of boy scouts and girl guides was taken
by the school physics master, Mr. Arie Kroch, later Israel's
Chief Scout, to a summer camp at Metulla. We pitched our
tents in a pleasant clearing surrounded by olive trees and
after we had been to see the imposing waterfall called the
Chimney, one of my father's childhood haunts, we embarked on a strenuous schedule of hikes.

Metulla, jutting into Lebanon and close to the Syrian
border, was ideally situated for hikes into foreign territory.
Our aim was to see the rivers Banias, Litani, Hasbani, and
Dan, all of which were entirely or predominantly outside
the boundaries of mandatory Palestine. Accordingly it was
arranged with the British frontier police that we should be
allowed to cross the border on the morning of each hike
and recross the same evening. There was nothing unusual
about the arrangement since Metulla villagers, whose fruit
orchards straddled the border, had long been allowed to do
just that.

The day we had been to see the Litani we stopped as
usual on the Lebanese side of the checkpoint and waited to
be counted and let through. The morning duty officer had

finished his shift and gone off. His Arab relief knew nothing of an arrangement. All he could see was a contingent of youngsters in military-type uniform led by a suspicious-looking individual wearing glasses and a whistle. The officer came out towards us with his hand pointedly resting on the holster of his pistol.

"Where do you think you are going?" he barked.

"Back to camp."

"Camp?" It was even more suspicious than he had imagined. "Where is camp?"

"At Metulla."

"Aha! You wish to enter Palestine."

"We want to go back to Metulla."

It was sorted out in the end, thanks either to Mr. Kroch's ability to produce convincing evidence that we were no illegal immigrants or, just as likely, to the melting effect of Rachel, our very attractive gym mistress. After that incident a young British police officer took to riding into camp and inquiring of Rachel whether everything was well with us. When she told him that a hike was scheduled to yet another river outside the border, he insisted on escorting us. All that hot day, as we were slowly following a trail towards the river, too exhausted to talk, he rode with us on his beautiful white horse, chatting to Rachel and vainly offering her a lift. I thought his assiduousness was purely amorous, but a few days later I began to wonder whether he had not been acting partly on instructions, trying to make sure we were not smuggling in illegal immigrants.

The term "illegal immigrants" was new in my vocabulary, having come into use mainly after Hitler's rise to power in 1933, when the number of people wishing to settle in Palestine far exceeded the legal quota. Some came in as tourists and stayed on, others entered the country through unguarded frontiers. Once in, they were absorbed into the comparative safety of the cities and the larger kibbutzim, where tracking them down was difficult in spite of surprise police raids.

Haifa's original landing place in the German Colony
before the building of the port

The *Lancastrian Prince* inaugurating the port of Haifa
on October 31, 1933
(Courtesy Press Department, Furness Withy Group)

Yehuda Bourla

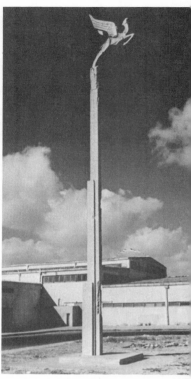

The Flying Camel at
the 1934 Levant Fair
(Photo Joseph Lee-Or)

Arabs punting in 1935
in the now-drained
Hula Lake *(Courtesy
Jewish National Fund
Picture Collection)*

Toscanini at the Dead Sea
(Courtesy Israel Philharmonic Orchestra Archives)

Toscanini (center left) and Huberman
after the inaugural concert of the
Palestine Orchestra in Tel Aviv on
October 26, 1936 *(Courtesy Israel
Philharmonic Orchestra Archives)*

Mordechai Golinkin,
founder of the
Palestine Opera
*(Courtesy Central
Library of Music and
Dance)*

Kibbutz Ramat Hakovesh in 1937
(Courtesy Jewish National Fund Picture Collection)

The refugee ship *Assimi*, 1939
(Courtesy Hagana Archives)

Metulla was a convenient point of entry for illegal immigrants coming from Syria and Lebanon, for access could be gained through the surrounding hills, which were a no-man's-land. Staying on, however, was risky. The village was tiny and a stranger crossing its only street could be spotted immediately. An illegal immigrant's only chance was to be concealed for a day or two in a friendly house and then driven inland through the main checkpoint at Rosh Pina, preferably by a local who had a chance of not being stopped. The British police were aware of what was going on and had offered a reward for information leading to the arrest of illegal immigrants; camp gossip had it that a certain Metulla farmer turned boarding house keeper had indeed betrayed some of his lodgers for a price. We spoke of him as the Traitor.

I did not need to be told anything when I noticed that the unoccupied tent meant to serve as a sick bay had its flaps down one day; like everyone else in camp, I just knew. After a day or two of secret comings and goings my friend Zephyra and I were informed that we had been selected to help smuggle two illegal immigrants through the Rosh Pina checkpoint, some twenty-five miles inland. We were the youngest in camp, looked even younger than our years, and could be passed off as the daughters of our charges.

At two in the afternoon a car drew up as near to the camp as the uneven dirt track would allow. The flaps of the tent were opened and the two men came out. One was wearing a dark woolen three-piece suit of the kind that no one in Palestine wore even at the height of winter; the other wore a similar suit of a slightly lighter color. Both held briefcases in their hands. They looked about thirty and I decided to adopt the man in the dark suit as my father. We did not talk to them nor they to us.

The driver explained that in the early afternoon, when the heat was at its most oppressive, the guards posted on the hills overlooking the main road would be too sapped of energy to come down towards us and climb up again, and might just wave us on. The four of us settled in the back of the car and tried to look like parents and children on a family outing. Soon we were on the smooth asphalt road leading to Rosh Pina and beyond. As we passed our first Arab village on the right the driver put out his hand and waved. The guard on top of the hill waved us on. The same thing happened when we passed by the second Arab village on the left. The road was now clear as far as Rosh Pina.

Even from a distance we could see that the barrier at the checkpoint was permanently down. A British officer and a local policeman walked slowly towards us as we stopped.

"Documents," the policeman said in English with a pronounced native accent. There were no identity cards in Palestine before the war.

The driver produced his driving license. The policeman passed it on to the officer who flipped through it and returned it to the policeman, who handed it back to the driver. Then the questioning began.

"Who are these people with you?"

"Holiday makers, sir. I'm showing them around the countryside."

The officer opened the back door of the car and said quietly to the man in the dark suit, "What's your name?"

"Yampulski." I never understood why a man who looked so obviously levantine should have chosen a Polish-sounding name.

"Where are you from?"

"Tel Aviv."

"Your address?"

"Allamby Street." Any child knew that Tel Aviv's Allenby Street was a shopping center, not a residential address. The officer turned to the man in the light suit: "And where are you from?"

"Tel Aviv."

"Your address?"

"Allamby Street."

The four of us were made to get out of the car. "I'm

detaining you for further questioning," the officer said to the two men. "You now," he turned to me. "What's your name?"

"Ruthi," I said sweetly, trying to act the innocent little girl out with her Daddy.

"Come on, surname as well."

"You'd better tell him," the driver said in Hebrew under his breath.

I told him.

"What does your father do?"

"He's a teacher."

"What's his address?"

"Ratchkovsky's House, Pevsner Street, Hadar Hacarmel, Haifa."

The officer winced. "And what's your name?" he asked Zephyra.

"Zephyra Barlass."

"What does your father do?"

"He's a teacher."

"What's his address?"

"Ratchkovsky's House, Pevsner Street, Hadar Hacarmel, Haifa."

The information we gave was perfectly correct but under the circumstances the coincidence of both address and father's occupation being identical sounded too much like a prearranged alibi. Before the officer had a chance to explode, the red-haired policeman who until then had kept silent, said without being asked, "I know that girl's father, sir." He pointed to me. "He was my teacher at school."

Zephyra and I were discharged. To convince the officer that we were indeed on a sight-seeing tour the driver took us past the barrier into Rosh Pina, bought us two glasses of ice-cold *gazoz*, and left us to look around. About an hour later he picked us up and drove us back to camp. Not long afterwards we read that two illegal immigrants caught at Rosh Pina had been deported to Syria.

Cases of deportation were regularly reported in the

press and each fresh case strengthened the general determination to resist the British government's immigration policy which had departed from the principle of absorptive capacity and was apparently based on a desire to appease the Arabs. An added grievance was the seemingly unrestricted entry into Palestine of illegal Arab immigrants from the Hauran region of Trans-Jordan. A popular magazine came out with a cartoon showing a shabby-looking Arab peasant with a goat, being stopped by a British soldier at a lonely checkpoint along the frontier.

"Who are you?" read the text underneath the cartoon. "Tourist? Immigrant? Have you got an Immigration Permit?"

"No *ya hawaja*, no sir. Me and my goat are from the Hauren."

"That's O.K. then. In you go."

A report presented by Britain to the League of Nations stated that 712 Jews were deported in 1934 out of a total of 2,347 illegal immigrants, most of whom were Hauranis. Such figures did not placate the *yishuv*. Hauranis did not belong in the Land of Israel; Jews did. Not a single Jew should have been deported; and every Jew who had the foresight to leave a hostile Europe and seek entry into Palestine should have been allowed to do so in order to rebuild his life in the Jewish National Home.

16

Back at Bat Galim

ALL THE YEARS we lived at Hadar Hacarmel mother took in lodgers to supplement her earnings. The flat at Lurie's House had three rooms. One was mother's bedroom *cum* study, where she gave Hebrew lessons to new immigrants, either individually or in groups of twos and threes. The second was the lodger's room, first occupied by a Syrian Arab, then by a young man from Hungary who worked on a building site, then by a doctor from Germany who required temporary accommodation while his house was being built, and finally by a Viennese lady and her small daughter. The daughter was as meek as a mouse but the mother used to clatter about the flat in her high-heeled slippers and start cooking on the noisy primus stove just as mother and I were sitting down to our supper in the shared kitchen. The third room was nominally mine, first shared with my brother until he left to live at father's, and then with a paying guest, a divorced lady from Eastern Europe who astonished me by splashing perfume all over her body instead of having a good wash under the shower.

Apart from a huge wardrobe which contained the family linen and everybody's clothes, my room had two divans, a large all-purpose table, a bookcase from which books had been banished in order to accommodate my roommate's cosmetics, and my piano. When I was not practicing sonatas by Haydn or Mozart, my friend Zephyra was brilliantly playing her two party pieces, Weber's *Invitation to the Dance* and Chopin's *Fantasie-Impromptu*. What with the two of us at the piano most afternoons, mother's students coming and going, lodgers cooking and entertaining, there was never a dull moment in the flat.

To add to the fun, mother had taken it into her head to give a start to a young artist, a new immigrant from Czechoslovakia, by commissioning him to paint my portrait. There I was in the midst of the general bustle, self-consciously occupying a chair in mother's room, clad in a fussy frock my sister had sent from Vienna, trying hard to look natural. Every now and then the doorbell was rung by one of my classmates, ostensibly calling to talk about homework but in reality to gape at artist and model. The finished portrait, I thought, looked nothing like me. The artist had gallantly ignored my protruding front teeth, which made it impossible for me to close my mouth properly, and endowed me with pretty pink lips and a serene expression. But mother was pleased and to my great embarrassment had the picture framed and hung above her desk, for all her students and visitors to see and admire.

One sultry summer day I mentioned that I had been having fits of dizziness. Mother put it down to my persistent refusal to touch any of the German dishes served at our new lunchtime eating place but, to be on the safe side, prescribed a good dosage of fresh sea air and announced that we should be spending the long vacation at Bat Galim.

The Bat Galim house had been made over to mother as part of the divorce settlement and was meant to be let unfurnished for as long as it was necessary for us to live in a rented flat within easy reach of my school. Most of the time, however, it was unoccupied. Every now and then we fastened to one of the shutters a new cardboard sign saying To Let instead of the one torn off by the sea breeze, and every now and then there was an unenthusiastic inquiry; most people wanted a modern flat, not an unmanageable two-story house. Returning for the summer to an unrentable property by the sea made good sense.

On the last day of term piano, bedding, tables, chairs,

the huge wardrobe, and a miscellany of domestic utensils were loaded on a mule-drawn cart which soon assumed the look and proportions of the Tower of Babylon. I rode with the driver while mother, tight-laced as usual and wearing a floppy hat against the sun, was left to make her own way by a succession of buses.

The seafront was as deserted as I had remembered it, only a barbed-wire fence blocked my favorite walk on the rocks; a large British army camp had been built on the outskirts of Bat Galim and the rocks formed its western boundary. The tamarisks and the palm trees had grown taller than ever and the fig tree was laden with fruit. The rest of the garden was completely covered with sand. I rushed into the kitchen to examine the old-fashioned charcoal oven although I knew it would never be lit again. Mother had brought along the latest thing, a primus stove with a silent burner. Like all its predecessors it was temperamental, and when not pumped at precisely the right moment, it ejected jets of paraffin which changed halfway up into columns of fire and soot. The old water pump was in good order, but there was no need to draw water from the garden well, for Bat Galim had been connected to the municipal water supply. We also had electricity.

The pleasant old routine by the sea was resumed, but now Bat Galim had an open-air swimming pool with a diving board. While Hadar Hacarmel visitors paid to get in through the turnstile, we Bat Galim youngsters sneaked in free by climbing over the protective sea wall. After a while I was persuaded to join a swimming class and transform my self-taught paddle into an elegant crawl.

The vacation at Bat Galim had been so beneficial that by the end of the summer mother was planning to resettle there permanently. My sister had married an architect from Vienna and was living with him in a rented one-room penthouse flat he himself had designed; my brother was studying forestry in California, and I was by now perfectly capable of commuting to school. Since the Bat Galim house was too large for just the two of us, mother had it converted into three self-contained flats and in due course we moved into one of them. For the first time in my life I had my own tiny room, my own desk, my own bookcase, and a gramophone with a collection of classical records. The other two flats, now that they were small and manageable, were easily let.

One of them was occupied for a while by Sergeant and Mrs. Cox. The sergeant had at first been stationed in the army camp near us, but when his young wife came over from England they were allowed to live out. The Coxes never referred to the accommodation as "our place" or "the flat"; it was always "our married quarters." Sometimes they invited me to have supper with them and afterwards put on a record and tried to teach me the foxtrot. Once or twice they took me to the camp cinema to see British or American films. Mrs. Cox lent me her copy of Mrs. Gaskell's *Cranford*, and when I opened it I saw that she had won it as a school prize.

Another tenant was a young American woman who had been working on a kibbutz before she came to live at Bat Galim. She lent me her copies of Cronin's *The Citadel* and Aldous Huxley's *Eyeless in Gaza*. There was also a Dutch couple, both very young, very blond, very frail, and very artistic, who said they were going to start the first puppet theater in Palestine.

Most of the tenants, however, had come from Germany. The German immigrants, or *Yekes* as they were nicknamed, pervaded every sphere of life. The inspector on the now streamlined Bat Galim bus service was a *Herr Doktor*, a dermatologist by profession; the dentist who put a brace on my teeth had come from Berlin; our home help was a bespectacled lady from Frankfurt who looked and spoke like a schoolmistress; and our fish supplier was a plump woman from Breslau who called three times a week, always at precisely the same time, with neatly sliced pieces of pond-bred carp wrapped in layers of ice.

The German immigrants were markedly different from any other national group we had absorbed so far. They spoke Hebrew, if they spoke it at all, with an excruciating accent and laced it with astounding grammatical combinations; they were punctual to a fault and expected everybody else to be the same; they said more thank-yous and pleases in a day than most of us did in a month of Sundays; and their table manners were extraordinary. Some of my new classmates moved me to indignation when they told me how in Germany their parents had made them sit down to meals with a book under each arm so that they should learn to eat with their elbows close to the body. The Palestinian way of eating, I informed them, was much more progressive; we put our elbows on the table.

Most of my mother's students were now German immigrants, professional men and women in their thirties and forties, who formally shook hands with her at the beginning and end of each lesson. One of them was horrified to find me sitting on the floor cracking almonds with my teeth; he said I put him in mind of the savages in the jungle. Next time he came for his lesson I made a point of crossing his line of vision with an ax slung over my shoulder.

The ax was part of our domestic equipment, used for chopping wood for the bathroom boiler. Every Friday afternoon I took it out of the cubbyhole and did battle on empty wooden crates discarded by the local greengrocer. I was reading Tennyson and the legends of the Round Table and liked to imagine myself hacking away at an enemy in defense of a helpless captive. With the sun in my eyes and my dark hair limply sticking to my forehead I saw myself as Lancelot:

> His broad clear brow in sunlight glow'd;
> On burnish'd hooves his war-horse trod;
> From underneath his helmet flow'd
> His coal-black curls as he rode,
> As he rode to Camelot.

I was inspired to write an Arthurian novel. There was a young knight called Sir James and a beautiful damsel called Ariel. Sir James had been captured and brave Ariel galloped out on her white steed to rescue him with her mighty sword. I was rather pleased with what I had written and read out the first chapter to my mother. To my surprise she looked troubled.

"This is a little like the story of St. Joan," she said. She had called her Jeanne d'Arc, in the French way.

"Who is Jeanne d'Arc?"

When she told me I felt I had been cheated out of a jolly good plot. I tore up the useless pages and after a phase of inactivity translated Oscar Wilde's short story "The Model Millionaire" and sent it off to a Tel Aviv weekly called *Nine P.M.* It was published under my name and several months later a pound note arrived for me by post. I then translated a short story by Prosper Mérimée called "La Perle de Tolède" and had it published in the same paper.

Translations were in great demand. Nowadays, when Hebrew has produced in S. Y. Agnon a co-winner of the Nobel Prize for literature and a number of other outstanding novelists whose books have been translated into English, it is perhaps difficult to imagine what a dearth of readable original fiction there was in Eretz Israel in the first three or four decades of the century. Yet a dearth there was. The novels of the mid-nineteenth-century visionaries like Mapu and Smolenskin who had revived a dead language were now archaic while later attempts at fiction were few and boringly didactic. At least that was how most young readers felt.

The detective stories of David Tidhar, the pen name of a Tel Aviv policeman who wrote with himself as the hero, were therefore all the rage when they first appeared in the early thirties. Published about once a week and costing something like a piaster, they bore such titles as "The Hangman of Corfu" or "The Black Hand" and were more thrilling than any Sherlock Holmes stories I had read in English. At school they were passed from hand to hand and since there was always a long waiting list, they were read during lessons under cover of an exercise book. My classmate Eli was caught reading one during a Hebrew literature lesson and was severely reprimanded.

The copy he was reading happened to be mine. During break I went up to the common room and asked to see the master.

"That book you have taken away from Eli is mine," I said with candor. "Please may I have it back?"

To my utter astonishment the master grew red in the face and shouted at the top of his voice: "You will never see this book again, not as long as I am literature master at this school. Get out of my sight!"

Nobody had ever told me or any of my friends that detective stories were forbidden reading. "Mr. Hienkin is a thief," I said furiously to my mother later that day. "He has stolen my book; he won't let me have it back. He's a thief thief thief!"

It was a happy day when scanning my father's bookshelves I came across a collection of short stories entitled *Sons of Arabia* by someone called Hawaja Moosa. It turned out to be the pen name of Moshe Smilansky, a well-known Rehovot farmer, born in the Ukraine in 1874 and a Palestine pioneer at the age of sixteen. His stories were mostly based on his intimate knowledge of the Arab way of life before the First World War and gave me an insight into a strange and fascinating world. I marveled at Bedouin superstitions, felt for the doomed love between an Arab village girl and a Jewish teacher, shed a tear for an idealistic Russian proselyte who drowned in his beloved Jordan. Each story was a little gem, realistic in background, romantic in spirit, tragic in its inexorability.

The one outstanding novelist of the time, as I felt then and still feel today, was Yehuda Bourla, a writer of imagination and sensitivity, born in Jerusalem in 1886 of a family which had immigrated from Turkey to Palestine some three centuries earlier. When I first came to know Bourla—the person, not his books—I was still a toddler at Bat Galim, where he lived for a while with his pretty wife and children. He was a teacher at the Reali School and once, when I was older, he stood in for my regular Hebrew master who was unwell. I remember nothing of what Mr. Bourla taught us that day, but I came out of the classroom with shining eyes and a realization that I had been inspired as never before. Shortly afterwards he left to teach in Tel Aviv and I never met him again. His novels, however, were among the great reading pleasures of my youth.

Bourla was the first modern Hebrew novelist who wrote about the way of life of the Sephardi Jews, that is Jews who had been living for centuries in Middle Eastern countries and were steeped in oriental traditions. He described their folklore, superstitions, and conventions and, like the true artist that he was, he wove into that unfamiliar background the universal themes of love, conflict, and tragedy. *His Hated Wife* told the story of a man who loathed his wife but could not bring himself to divorce her because of his dependence on her wealth. *In Darkness Striving* followed the tortuous path of a philanderer who fell in love with a divorced Muslim woman, thus facing the double dilemma of his own failed marriage and the taboos of two religions. *Songstress* was an eye-opener about a professional entertainer who brought dignity to a dubious calling while *Daughter of Zion and Na'ama* described women in the grip of unacceptable love. Some of Bourla's heroines shocked me and momentarily outraged my rigid puritanism, but his blend of realism, romanticism, and tolerance was irresistible. He was a master storyteller, molding a developing language into patterns of beauty and freshness.

On the whole, however, we read translations of world classics or original works in any language we could. My own choice was much influenced by my French mistress

Madame Kalougai, wife of Professor Kalougai who taught chemistry at the Hebrew Technion. *La Kalougaitte*, as she was nicknamed, was a middle-aged lady with a pale face and coarse thinning hair dyed pitch black. She was usually dressed in light-colored blouses and loose skirts and left behind a whiff of refreshing scent. During the summer she carried a parasol and when confronted by a train of donkeys taking a shortcut through the school grounds she would poke them with its tip and brush past them murmuring in French, *"Pardon, pardon."*

Madame Kalougai was noted for her infinite patience with her students. With me she took extra care, giving up some of her free time to teach me things which were way beyond the school curriculum. Thanks to her I was reading French for pleasure at fifteen and coaching younger pupils for pocket money at sixteen. During my final years at school she handed out to me whatever was available at the school library in the way of Stendhal, Lamartine, Benjamin Constant, Voltaire, Chateaubriand, George Sand, Flaubert, Maupassant, Duhamel, Daudet.

It was partly at her instigation that I started keeping a diary and filled it with comments on books I had read. I commented in English on English books, in French on French books, and in Hebrew—for want of enough original books inspiring comment—on boyfriends and daily occurrences.

One of my Hebrew entries for January 1936 read as follows: "Seen a radio set at Café Companietz in Herzl Street. Interesting."

It was of course much more than "interesting." It was enthralling; it was something I had never seen before. However, like many a young girl who keeps a diary with an eye to an anonymous reader, I kept mine partly for myself and partly for a Prince Charming—a trilingual one of course—who would one day discover the beauty of my soul through a surreptitious reading of my entries. It was therefore essential not to show myself up as a country bumpkin gaping at a radio set, but appear to be a sophisticated schoolgirl who took technological innovations in her stride. "Interesting" struck just the right balance.

Radio was a foreign word not much in use before the affluent immigrants of the early thirties brought over their German-made radio sets along with their heavy furniture, their pianos, their gramophones, and their collections of classical records. Even then nobody was quite sure what to call those elaborately carved wooden boxes which produced music from Europe at the turn of a knob. Hebrew technical terms were still arbitrary and imprecise. Radio sets were called radio machines and listeners who wished to improve shortwave reception were earnestly advised to fix a "record" on their rooftops. It was only after Palestine had a radio station of its own that an acceptable word for *aerial* was thought up and the word *record* assigned to denote a disc spinning at 78 rpm.

The Palestine Broadcasting Service was introduced in 1936 by the British government for the edification and entertainment of the people of the country and was modeled on the tradition and expertise of the BBC. Opening day was awaited with a mixture of curiosity and condescension. New immigrants who had heard radio programs abroad and could pick up European stations on their imported radio sets wondered what cultural contribution a Palestine station could make, while older residents and young natives looked forward to witnessing a miracle of technology. Even before the inaugural transmission was put on the air, the government had to face its first broadcasting crisis.

The new station was to transmit six or seven hours a day, seven days a week, in the three official languages of the country. That much was perfectly acceptable to all sections of the population. What was not acceptable to the Jewish community however was the proposed name of the station. It was all very well for the English language programs to identify it as the Palestine Broadcasting Service, for Palestine was the proper name of the country in English, but it was unthinkable that the station should be identified on the Hebrew language programs as the Broadcasting Service of *Palestina*. For one thing *Palestina* was not a Hebrew word; for another its use offended patriotic pride. The only way to identify the new radio station in plain Hebrew was as the Broadcasting Service of Eretz Israel.

That demand was unacceptable to the government, for Eretz Israel was not the official name of the country. It was Palestine (EI). In the end a compromise formula was found. The name of the country was left out altogether from both Hebrew and Arabic announcements, and the name of the city where Broadcasting House was situated was introduced instead. Thus the British-controlled Palestine Broadcasting Service came to be officially known in Hebrew as *Kol Yerooshalayim*, the Voice of Jerusalem, while the Arab-language programs opened with the equally patriotic identification of *Hoona Al Koods*, Al Koods being the traditional Muslim name for the Holy City.

Inauguration day, March 30, 1936, fell on a Monday, one of the two days in the week when I had afternoon classes and therefore could not be near a radio set in time for the 4:15 P.M. opening. By the time I reached the house of a friend whose parents had a set I had missed the introductory words of the Postmaster General, the official opening by the High Commissioner Sir Arthur Grenfell Wauchope, and a concert played live by the band of the 2nd Battalion of the Queen's Cameron Highlanders. All I could hear was monotonous oriental music, of the kind I often heard emanating from old gramophones in the Arab cafés of the Old City. I thought I had picked up the wrong station when an attractive female voice announced in Hebrew that we had been listening to a live performance by the resident Oriental Ensemble which consisted of a flute, a tambourine, two violins, and three other string instruments known only by their Arabic names of *ood, kanoon,* and *santoor.* This was followed by Hebrew songs and an impassioned rendering of excerpts from H. N. Bialik's *The Scroll of Fire* by Hanna Rovina, *Habima* Theater's first lady. The last item on the first day's program consisted of dance music from England, relayed through the BBC Empire Service (today's World Service).

In the following weeks and months there were frequent relays from England, such as the Oxford-Cambridge boat race and the England-Scotland football match from Wembley Stadium. On April 30, when the short-lived third Levant Fair was opened in Tel Aviv, the BBC Empire Service relayed from London a congratulatory speech by the Secretary of State for the Colonies. Such relays strengthened the feeling that Palestine, whatever its political status, was part of the mighty British Empire. At school my form was taking a course called the History of the British Empire with Trevelyan as required reading. I became familiar with such terms as crown colonies, dominions, tariffs, and the white man's burden. King Edward VIII's romance with Mrs. Simpson was no gossip item but a constitutional crisis which was anxiously followed. The day after the abdication, on December 11, 1936, the news was splashed in banner headlines all over the front page of *Ha'aretz,* the country's leading Hebrew daily. It made no difference that in the shock of the moment the headline had been misprinted: KING EDWARD V ABDICATES.

After mother had bought a powerful Austrian radio set—there were no *totzeret ha'aretz* ones as yet—Britain became even more tangible. There was a place on the dial marked Daventry which during the summer months broadcast orchestral music called Promenade Concerts; Tuesday was Wagner night and Friday Beethoven night. I was discovering other stations as well. Hilversum was good for classical music, Bari sometimes broadcast in

Arabic, Bucharest and Milano had lady announcers with attractive voices, and French stations had a funny way of presenting news bulletins in two voices, a man's alternating with a woman's. Once I picked up a German voice speaking hysterically and what sounded like a huge crowd chanting, *"Sieg Heil Sieg Heil Sieg Heil."*

With the establishment of a Hebrew radio station an exciting new vocabulary was coming into being. Radio remained *radio*, but now there were words for broadcasting, male and female announcers, time signal, and relay station. The main Hebrew news bulletin of the day, at 7:55 P.M., helped to disseminate recently coined words which had not yet been widely absorbed. Tourists, I now knew, no longer "fluttered" by aeroplanes but "flew" in them; an aeroplane no longer "set sail" but "took off"; and a place where lunches were served was no longer a "food house" but a "restaurant."

Another exciting innovation was the regular transmission of recorded music. There was a great deal of Beethoven, Mozart, Haydn, and Schubert, a fair amount of Liszt and Wagner, and a sprinkling of hitherto unfamiliar composers like Purcell and Byrd. The habit of listening to classical music on 78 rpm records spread from radio to community halls and became an accepted form of public entertainment. For a piaster or two I could gain admittance to Haifa's Culture Hall and join the regulars for the weekly performance of a symphony or a violin concerto on a manual gramophone. Every three and a half minutes or so there was a screech and a break, during which the audience waited with bated breath for a record to be turned over or changed. Fortunately music lovers had something more satisfying in store for them. Before 1936 was out one of the greatest events in the country's musical history had taken place: the founding of the Palestine Orchestra, later renamed the Israel Philharmonic Orchestra.

17

≈

Toscanini

MOST MUSIC LOVERS will probably know that the Palestine
Orchestra was founded by Bronislaw Huberman and inaugurated by Arturo Toscanini. But not many music lovers, born into societies where symphony orchestras are an
established part of the cultural environment, will perhaps
realize what an extraordinary impact its founding in 1936
made on a population yearning for a taste of European
culture in the midst of a harsh struggle for its very existence. The orchestra was manna from Heaven. It opened a
window to a world of enchantment and fantasy which not
many of the older generation, and none of us young natives, had ever glimpsed before.

It was the Polish-born Jewish violinist Bronislaw
Huberman who first thought of establishing in Palestine a
symphony orchestra consisting of Jewish musicians fleeing from the gathering storm in Europe. When Hitler rose
to power in January of 1933, Huberman called on fellow
musicians to boycott performances in Germany and in July
of that year he turned down an invitation to give a series of
concerts with the Berlin Philharmonic, explaining his action in a letter to the press which was published in New
York, Paris, and Prague. That summer he met Arturo Toscanini who had already declined to conduct at Bayreuth,
and an understanding was established. The following year
Huberman began to campaign for his idea. He himself had
given a recital in Palestine as early as 1929 and had good

reason to believe that a professional orchestra, performing on a regular basis, would fill a need; but even he had not guessed how deep the need was and how widespread.

His project struck a chord in many hearts. Palestine Orchestra committees were set up in several countries and a fund was started. When contributions, particularly from American supporters, had assured the orchestra's existence for an initial period of three years, Huberman approached Toscanini and asked him to conduct the inaugural concert in Tel Aviv. Asking the world's greatest conductor to travel thousands of miles to conduct an orchestra which had not yet come into being and whose potential was unknown was as bold as it was inspired. Toscanini not only accepted but waived his fee and even his traveling expenses.

Preparations were long and strenuous. Musicians had to be auditioned, immigration permits applied for, a répétiteur engaged to mold the orchestra into a cohesive musical entity. In December 1936 Toscanini at long last arrived in Palestine, his name preceding him like a pillar of fire, and the gratitude of the *yishuv* spread before him like a thick carpet. The country was already in the throes of the Arab Revolt, with murderous attacks on Jewish settlements and inter-urban buses an everyday occurrence; for a little while worrying about the political outcome of the violence was set aside. The greatest event of the day was Toscanini's arrival to launch the Palestine Orchestra.

If for the layman the sixty-nine-year-old Toscanini was a legendary conductor whose stand against Fascism and Nazism had made him all the more revered, for the newly recruited members of the orchestra he was a formidable genius whose reputation for perfectionism had put fear in the doughtiest of hearts. Before the first rehearsal everybody was in a state, musicians, *répétiteur* and Huberman. Toscanini arrived at the Tel Aviv rehearsal hall, made straight for the podium and without a word of preamble began conducting Brahms's Second Symphony. At the end of the rehearsal he declared himself satisfied. The musicians were incredulous. At the end of the second rehearsal he said nothing. The musicians were despondent. During the third rehearsal he lost his temper and thundered in every language he knew. The musicians were exuberant. At last they were being treated like a professional orchestra.

Communication presented some difficulty. Most of the musicians had played in leading orchestras in Western Europe and had been used to working in German. Toscanini spoke a mixture of German, French, and English which none of the players could easily follow. Huberman suggested communicating by sign language, Toscanini was prepared to try anything. As the orchestra was rehearsing the Salterello from Mendelssohn's Italian Symphony he put down his baton, rolled up his trousers, and started hopping about to demonstrate how dancelike the music should be. After the rehearsal he did not mince his words. "You are too Prussian for my liking," he managed to say in his mixture of languages. "Don't play me Prussian marches. Play lightly, like the French, like the Italians." The musicians were stunned; their idea of perfection was the sound of the Berlin Philharmonic.

The inaugural concert was held on Saturday, December 26, 1936, in one of the barnlike auditoriums of the Levant Fair grounds in Tel Aviv. That December was one of the coldest within living memory. Wearing galoshes, heavy overcoats smelling of mothballs, scarves and improvised headgear, thousands of people had queued up in the rain and wind to pay the unheard-of price of sixty piasters for the cheapest seat. While the three thousand lucky ones were waiting excitedly in their seats, several hundred others stood in the cold outside the hall, hoping to catch the strains of music through the thin wall.

It was a long program, consisting of Brahms's Second

Symphony, Rossini's *The Silken Ladder* Overture, Schubert's Unfinished Symphony, the Nocturne and Scherzo from Mendelssohn's *Midsummer Night's Dream* and Weber's *Oberon* Overture. In the midst of the tumultuous applause at the end of the evening Huberman was heard to say: "Bringing together seventy-two Jewish musicians was hard enough; turning them from seventy-two self-confirmed soloists into a disciplined orchestra was a feat."

The inaugural program was repeated in Jerusalem's Edison Film Theater and in Haifa's newly built Armon Film Theater. Since the Armon was situated on a noisy main road it was not the ideal venue for a symphony concert, but the local bus company and the Haifa municipality came gallantly to the rescue. The day before the concert I read the following announcement on the front page of *Ha'aretz*:

> The Palestine Orchestra Society hereby notifies the public that the orchestral concert conducted by A. Toscanini at the Armon Thursday on 31 December (tomorrow), will begin at 8 P.M. sharp and no one will be allowed into the auditorium after the scheduled time. The doors will open to the public at 7:15 P.M. and bus traffic outside the theater will be suspended from 7:15 P.M. until after the conclusion of the concert.

The suspension of a public service, proof of Haifa's reverence for culture, became standard practice for many years to come. As for the concert, it was described by all who had attended it as galvanizing, stupendous, historic, the performance of a lifetime. Few wondered why the intermission, scheduled to last half an hour, had lasted a full hour and a half, but nobody was unduly inquisitive. Perhaps the maestro had needed a little extra rest between symphonies; perhaps he had been slow getting rid of all those dignitaries who had streamed backstage to pay their respects; or perhaps it was just the mysterious way in which symphony concerts were conducted. It was only many years after Toscanini's death that I learned what had actually taken place behind the footlights on that extraordinary evening.

The concert had begun well. There was no reason to fear any mishap and after the Rossini overture the orchestra launched confidently into Brahms's Second Symphony. The first movement went smoothly and so did the second. Then the inconceivable happened. The first trumpet player had somehow got distraught and while the orchestra began playing the third movement he plunged headlong into the fourth. Toscanini nearly went up in smoke. He glared daggers at the trumpeter, cursed *sotto voce* in Italian, took the work faster and faster and brought it to an end in a blaze of fury, *prestissimo* and *fortissimo*. Never had there been such a frenzied climax, never had there been such frenetic applause. Before it died down Toscanini stormed out, knocking down a couple of music stands on the way, and refused to go on with the second half of the concert. It took all of an hour and a half to coax him back on stage. The audience had suspected nothing.

Toscanini's generosity to the *yishuv* was unbounded. Seeing that the public thirst for music had not nearly been quenched by his three scheduled concerts, he agreed to rehearse and conduct an unscheduled all-Beethoven program. Again it was performed in the three main cities and again there were determined queues before each concert. The whole country had gone music mad. "Nobody discusses the unusually icy weather, the storms, the driving rain, or the heavy snowfall in Jerusalem, Safed, and Hebron," ran a press comment. "Even the sessions of the Royal Commission [the Peel Commission] with their anti-Jewish and anti-Zionist undertones have been momentarily forgotten. The talk of the day is orchestra, Huberman, and Toscanini."

In the first week of January 1937 Toscanini took the orchestra on its first foreign tour, conducting before packed houses in Cairo and Alexandria. There they parted, but not before Toscanini had promised to come back to Palestine as soon as possible. The orchestra returned from its Egyptian tour laden with honors and the Hebrew press coined a phrase which was to become as familiar as the first verse in Genesis: "The Palestine Orchestra is the best in the Middle East." I read it with pride and repeated it with conviction. Several years had passed before it occurred to me that I had never heard of symphony orchestras in such countries as Egypt, Syria, Lebanon, Trans-Jordan, Iraq, Kuwait, or Saudi-Arabia. The Palestine Orchestra could hardly have qualified as "the best in the Middle East" when it was surely the only one.

I heard it in Haifa during its very first season, at the beginning of 1937, under Issay Dobrowen. Tickets for non-Toscanini concerts were not prohibitively expensive, but a system of advance subscription for the entire season made them hard to get on a single-booking basis. Mine came to me by sheer good luck. The Reali School Arabic master, a distinguished Orientalist from Germany, was unable to attend one of the subscribers' concerts and offered his ticket for sale in the common room. My father promptly paid him twelve and a half piasters and gave me the precious present during morning break.

When the day came I sat small and tense on my wooden chair at the Armon Theater, waiting for the gates of heaven to open. Everybody was dressed up to the nines, women in bright-colored gowns and heavy jewelry, men in suits and ties. Nobody was in a hurry. People strolled casually down the aisles looking for friends, took their time settling into their seats, waved their programs to acquaintances just spotted on the other side of the auditorium. The musicians wandered on stage one by one or in groups, started tuning up, and tried out little phrases at full volume, competing with the general hubbub. At last the conductor came on, acknowledged the perfunctory applause, and turned his back to us. The lights dimmed but no hush fell; instead there rose a last-minute wave of coughing and throat clearing. The conductor, who had already raised his baton, dropped his arms, waited, raised them again. The music engulfed me.

I was not familiar with any of the works performed that evening, but neither were most members of the audience during that first season of the Palestine Orchestra. To avoid the embarrassment of premature applause we did not start clapping until the astonished conductor had turned to face us and made his first bow. The applause, I noticed, was at its loudest before the intermission and at its most perfunctory after the final work of the evening, when people were fretting to catch their buses. The bus company had thoughtfully stationed dozens of empty buses in a side street for the convenience of concert-goers, but there was a scramble to get on first all the same.

In April 1938 Toscanini returned to Palestine for another series of concerts, disregarding the risk involved in coming to a country where Arab violence had been taking a heavy toll for two years. This time opening night was held in Haifa. Huberman, the father of the orchestra, had arrived by ship a few days earlier; Mrs. Weizmann came down from Rehovot with a party of titled ladies and gentlemen from England; the commander of the French mandatory forces in Syria had driven over from Damascus. The Armon Theater was aglitter. The orchestra, with fifteen months' experience behind it and discreetly reinforced for the duration of the maestro's visit by the first trumpeter of the Vienna Philharmonic, played as never before. Schubert's Seventh Symphony brought the house down. A day or two later I read that the concert had started somewhat inauspiciously. The stolid Haifaites, relying on the good old tradition of unpunctuality, had turned up late and were astounded to find doors locked and admission refused until the intermission.

When the same program was repeated in Jerusalem, Schubert's Seventh Symphony was broadcast live from the Edison Theater. That evening the usually crowded streets of Tel Aviv and Haifa were deserted. People huddled around radio sets at friends' houses and in cafés, as well as in communal halls in kibbutzim and villages, in order to hear what everybody sensed was musical history in the making, a live broadcast of the Palestine Orchestra conducted by Toscanini. One of the country's leading music critics later took the Palestine Broadcasting Service to task for having broadcast only part of the concert and, above all, for having lacked the foresight to record it for rebroadcast and posterity.

As on his previous visit, Toscanini generously agreed to conduct a second program in the three main cities. Since my birthday roughly coincided with the date of the Haifa performance, my sister and her husband pooled their resources and bought me an expensive present in the form of a ticket for what turned out to be the last concert Toscanini was to conduct in Palestine.

It was held at Haifa's Armon Theater on Tuesday, April 26. This time everybody was ensconced in their seats well before 8:30 and the only delay was caused by the prolonged applause which welcomed the seventy-one-year-old conductor as he made his way to the podium. The sensation of the evening was Toscanini's interpretation of the preludes to Acts I and III of Wagner's *Lohengrin*. Used as I was to hearing Wagner's music dismissed as loud and blustering, I was deeply moved by the preludes in the sensitive rendering of the orchestra's string section. At the end of the evening we went berserk, for once forgetting about buses, clapping madly, cheering, bringing Toscanini back five times. The following day he left Haifa by air, never to return. His eight April concerts had been attended by 20,000 people.

Toscanini's 1938 visit had an unexpected sequel. Long before his arrival a public controversy had been raging about the propriety of performing in Palestine works by a composer such as Wagner whose fierce anti-Jewish views were identifiable with modern Nazism. After Toscanini's delicate interpretation it was tacitly agreed that Wagner had some good in him and that he could be performed by Jews for Jews despite his professed anti-Semitism. In June 1938 Yasha Hornstein conducted the Palestine Orchestra in Wagner's *Tannhäuser* Overture, and in July Bronislaw Schultz conducted the *Flying Dutchman* Overture. In November of that year Eugen Szenker was billed to conduct the *Mastersinger* Overture. By then, however, Germany had committed one of its worst atrocities against Jews and the mood of tolerance towards Wagner had changed.

The atrocity was the last act of a drama which began on November 7, when a seventeen-year-old Jewish lad sought to avenge the suffering of his people by shooting a German diplomat in Paris. Two days later the diplomat died of his wounds and Nazi Germany took its revenge. On the night of November 9 thousands of Jewish shops and hundreds of synagogues were burned down, Jews were beaten to death and 20,000 were sent to concentration camps. It came to be known as the Crystal Night or the Night of the Broken Glass.

The news of the atrocities began to trickle in on November 10 and was splashed in the Hebrew press the next day. Szenker's opening concert in Tel Aviv was held on November 12. As a tense audience was waiting for him to come on, a spokesman for the management stepped on the stage and announced that in response to hundreds of requests Wagner would not be performed that evening. There was a complete hush, then a woman burst into uncontrollable sobs. Wagner was taken off the Palestine Orchestra's repertoire once and for all.

That year Huberman came back to play with the orchestra, having miraculously survived a plane crash and injury to his fingers. In February 1940 he came yet again, finding the *yishuv* deeply involved in the struggle for immigration and the war effort but as keen as ever to hear good music. That month an earthquake in Turkey had claimed many victims and rendered thousands of people homeless. Huberman and the orchestra went to Cairo to give a charity performance in aid of the Turkish homeless, under the auspices of the Red Crescent and King Farouk of Egypt. At a press conference held just before setting out for Cairo Huberman expressed what most of us felt and hoped for. "Our concert," he said, "would demonstrate in the clearest way the mission of music as an instrument of international goodwill. It would also be evidence of the will of Palestine to share the misfortunes as well as the joys of the neighboring countries."

PART
THREE
Days of Wrath

Save the nation! Save the nation!
What with? Ask not; with whatever we find.
Who with? Question not; with whoever volunteers,
Touched by his people's plight.
The defenders are assembling, stand not apart.
Any sacrifice's acceptable, any gift a true one,
No questioning in times of danger.

H. N. Bialik, 1873–1934

18

Doing My Bit

THE MORNING OF APRIL 19, 1936, began as usual. It was a Sunday, which meant that it was the first working day after the Sabbath break. By eight o'clock the town traffic was in full hooting force, shops were open for business, and I was at my school desk dutifully listening to the math master sort out an equation I had got wrong. Nobody had any reason to regard the date as anything special except me, for it was my birthday. By the evening, however, April 19 had become engraved on the pages of history as a day of riots and killing, marking the beginning of what came to be known as the Arab Revolt.

The outbreak was part of a coordinated Arab effort to stop Jewish immigration and the turning of Palestine into a Jewish National Home in the spirit of the Balfour Declaration. Indeed immigration, to the joy of the *yishuv* and the alarm of the Arabs, had been growing by leaps and bounds. In 1932 only 9,553 immigrants came to Palestine on legal permits; in 1933, after Hitler's rise to power, the figure shot up to 30,327. In 1934 it rose to 42,359 and in 1935 to 61,844. Even though the entire Jewish population of Palestine in 1936 was only 400,000, the Arab majority had dwindled since the beginning of the British Mandate from 90 percent to 70 percent. The Arab leaders were determined not only to stop the trend but to reverse it.

The *casus belli* was, as before, only a pretext. This time it was a rumor in Jaffa about Tel Aviv mourners killing two

Arabs as retaliation for the earlier killing of two Jews. While unsuspecting Jewish shopkeepers were waiting for customers in their shops on the Tel Aviv-Jaffa border, an incited Arab mob stormed in, killing, wounding, ransacking, and setting buildings on fire. That same evening High Commissioner Wauchope issued an official communiqué, the first of many:

April 19, 9 P.M.

The High Commissioner regrets to announce that disturbances occurred in Jaffa this morning involving several casualties.

Owing to false rumours (which were at once officially contradicted) that Arabs had been killed, crowds assembled about eleven o'clock in the Manshia Quarter of Jaffa and disturbances arose in the course of which several attacks were made upon Jews.

The police intervened promptly and by the early afternoon order was restored and the situation was completely under control.

The casualties, so far as is known, were as follows: seven Jews were killed, eleven seriously injured and 23 slightly injured. Three rounds in all were fired under the direct control of Superior Police Officers after due warning had been given, one round when a crowd refused to disperse and two rounds in order to stop a murderous assault already in progress. The deaths of the two Arabs mentioned above as killed resulted from these shots.

As a precautionary measure the Defence Order in Council had been proclaimed, empowering the High Commissioner to put Emergency Regulations into operation and a Curfew Regulation has accordingly been imposed at Jaffa and Tel Aviv requiring the inhabitants to be within doors between 7 P.M and 5 P.M.

No incidents are reported from any other part of the country.

By the following day, when all the Jewish casualties had been counted, the death toll had risen to sixteen; nor was the situation as under control as the communiqué had stated. It was to remain violent and bloody for three whole years.

Soon after the Jaffa outbreak the Arabs called a general strike hoping to paralyze the country's economy. A newly elected Arab Higher Committee informed the British government that the strike would go on indefinitely unless Jewish immigration was stopped, the transfer of land from Arabs to Jews prohibited, and a Palestinian government based on majority rule set up. At the same time a campaign of terror was launched; Jewish settlements were attacked, Jewish property was set on fire, Jewish inter-urban buses were sniped at, newly planted forests were uprooted.

At first nobody anticipated that the "disturbances," as the official communiqué called them, would last more than a week or two. At the beginning of May the talk of the day shifted to the Italian aggression in Abyssinia and the flight to Jerusalem of Emperor Haile Selassie and his family. Our hearts went out to the Lion of Judah, scion of the brief amour between King Solomon and the Queen of Sheba at the time of her state visit to Jerusalem two thousand years earlier. My sister was moved to write the Emperor a letter of sympathy, assuring him of the hospitality of her country. I already visualized her being summoned to Jerusalem to receive a token of imperial gratitude when she admitted that she had written anonymously.

That same month we heard on the newly inaugurated Voice of Jerusalem that Britain had appointed a Royal Commission under Lord Peel to investigate the whole Palestine issue. By then it was clear that the disturbances were no passing outburst, but in spite of the mounting death toll the Jewish leaders called on the *yishuv* to exercise *havlaga*, the virtue of self-restraint and nonretaliation. With such exhortation in mind those who could went about their business as usual. Two young men I knew, friends of my sister, left for Spain to join the International

Brigade fighting on the side of the Republicans in the Civil War. My history master talked of King Edward VIII and the abdication crisis. Everybody was talking about the forthcoming inauguration of the Palestine Orchestra by the legendary Toscanini.

Towards the end of the year the Royal Commission arrived in Jerusalem. By that time the Arab strike had been called off and attacks on Jewish settlements had subsided. Even so the strain of combining agricultural work with guard duties was beginning to tell. Schoolboys and girls in the upper forms were exhorted to spend their holidays working on the land in order to release adults for defense duties. The Passover vacation of 1937 thus found me and some of my schoolmates at Ramat Hakovesh, a young kibbutz near the Arab town of Kalkilia, which had been attacked several times.

I had not been to a kibbutz since the beginning of the Arab Revolt and was not altogether prepared for the siege conditions that now prevailed in every vulnerable settlement. Ramat Hakovesh was entirely surrounded by barbed-wire fence, and the tall water reservoir, traditionally a meeting place for nightly communal singing, now had an armed watchman on its roof. As we were let in through the only gate in the fence we were overtaken by two trucks packed with kibbutz members returning from a day's work in the outlying fields and orange groves. Some had spades and shears slung over their shoulders; others had guns. As night fell, the searchlight on top of the water tower began revolving.

After we had met fellow volunteers from Tel Aviv and Jerusalem schools, we were taken to our quarters. Kibbutz members lived in low wooden huts. We were allocated a two-story concrete building which had been left unfinished because manpower had been diverted to defense. The Haifa group, three girls and two boys, was allotted a room on the ground floor, with no doors, no electricity, no floor tiles, no plaster on the walls, and gaping holes for windows. On the other hand we had the unexpected luxury of five iron bedsteads with five palliasses. There was even a cupboard.

Most of the boys were assigned jobs in the fields and orange groves and left every morning in the trucks, returning well before sunset to the safety of the barbed-wire fence. Girls were mostly assigned duties within the enclosure. I was taken to the vegetable plot and shown how to dig, prepare beds, transfer seedlings, and irrigate. By midday I was so exhausted all I could do was crawl to the nearest skeleton of a building and sprawl flat on the cool concrete floor.

After a hard day's work it was good to take a cold shower and sit down to a meal at the long, rough tables in the dining hut. There were tureens with the soup of the day and large chunks of homemade bread which I devoured voraciously like everyone else. On the first evening we danced the *hora* under the starlit sky but the Haifa group soon gave it up in favor of a few quiet rounds of the Story Game. Five objects were chosen at random and each of us had to make up an installment featuring one of them. After a week we had exhausted our inventiveness and took to narrating other people's stories. One fellow told the story of Oscar Wilde's *The Picture of Dorian Gray,* which he had read in Hebrew; another told the story of Francesca da Rimini, which he had read in German; I told the story of Pierre Benoît's *L'Atlantide,* which I had read in French.

When it was time to go back to school the *kibbutznik* woman in charge of the vegetable plot called me to the potting shed and offered me two young cacti with pretty red flowers; one of them still flourishes on my sister's balcony in Haifa. There had been no attacks on Ramat Hakovesh while we were there, but during the following eighteen months it was attacked no fewer than forty times.

One morning before setting out for school I saw in the daily paper that one of the two trucks taking kibbutz members to the orange grove had driven over a mine and was blown up. Among the ten people killed were some I had come to know during my stay.

I never had occasion to return to Ramat Hakovesh, but some time in the mid-sixties I happened to pick up a volume which traced its history since its foundation. While turning the pages I came across a list of names, mine among them, with a handsome tribute to the youngsters who in the spring of 1937 gave a hand to a kibbutz under seige.

In the summer of that same year I went camping on Mount Carmel. This was no ordinary holiday camp. It had been organized by the Reali School to give pupils of the upper classes their first training in the art of self-defense. There were about thirty of us, some six girls and the rest boys, camping in a wooden hut in a secluded part of the range. We had strict orders to carry around a prescribed schoolbook so that if intercepted by a suspicious British security officer we could hastily squat under a tree and pretend to be studying in the open. As it happened the subterfuge was never put to the test.

I was given a Winchester rifle and taught how to take it apart and put it together again. I learned to take aim, shoot, throw dud hand grenades, scale walls, seek cover among the rocks, crawl in the open, and carry mock wounded in improvised stretchers. The emphasis was on *hagana*, defense; we were not to attack unless threatened. The moral inspiration came, I think, from the much quoted Talmudic dictum: "If someone approaches you with intent to kill, rise early to kill him."

Our chief trainer was a taciturn fellow in his late twenties or early thirties who went by the code name of Misha. Men who had access to illegal arms and taught Jewish youths the rudiments of self-defense were known as Instructors. When a visitor from England asked me what a certain young fellow was doing for a living, I therefore stated, "He's an Instructor."

"An instructor of what?"

I had not realized that an instructor could instruct anything other than the use of weapons and just repeated, "He's an Instructor."

"Where does he instruct?"

"All over the place."

"He's not attached to a school then?" Bernard was puzzled.

"Of course not."

"Can he live on it?"

"He's more likely to die of it," I snapped impatiently.

"What an extraordinary young lady you are," Bernard said.

I had never been called a young lady before and was momentarily pacified. For a while I forgave Bernard his pomaded black hair, his manicured fingernails, and his shiny black shoes. Bernard said that if I married him he would buy me a house on Brighton Beach and assured me that living there would be every bit as nice as living at Bat Galim.

"You would be a lovely wife to come home to," he said.

"How do you know I would be in when you got back home?"

"Where else would you be?"

"At my place of work."

"No wife of mine is going out to work," Bernard said proudly. "I can afford to keep a wife."

"No Palestinian-born girl will ever marry you," I retorted indignantly. "We don't want to be kept. We want to go out to work at our own chosen professions."

"You would have a car," Bernard said enticingly. "You would be able to drive everywhere."

"Don't want a car. I can walk."

"What an extraordinary young lady you are," he repeated, mistaking my rudeness for maidenly coyness. In the end mother obligingly reminded him that I was still a schoolgirl and that, much as we were honored by his attentions, it was only fair to point out that they were somewhat premature.

"What a lovely mother-in-law you would have made," Bernard said before going out of our life.

I was still at camp when the Peel Commission completed its inquiry into the Palestine maze and in July 1937 came up with the revolutionary proposal of partition. The idea was to divide Palestine into a Jewish state and an Arab state, leaving Britain in charge of Jerusalem and its environs. When the news reached us at camp we were dazed with the glory that nationhood held in store. It did not matter that the size of the proposed Jewish state was tiny; statehood was the highest prize imaginable. The Jewish leadership was less euphoric; some leaders had serious misgivings, while Weizmann and Ben-Gurion supported the plan as a lesser evil. The British government announced its readiness to accept the recommendations of the Peel Commission, but the Arab Higher Committee rejected the idea of partition outright and insisted on its original demands.

The Arab Revolt flared up again. For the next eighteen months it was impossible to open a daily paper without reading of fresh acts of violence; buses and convoys traveling between Tel Aviv and Jerusalem were sniped at from the hills, settlements were attacked, police stations raided, Jewish supernumerary policeman killed. In the summer of 1938 violence broke out just outside Haifa's Old City. Some hundred Jews going about their business were wounded, six were killed, and a curfew was imposed from dusk to dawn. When it was lifted ten days later, violence broke out again.

While British security forces fought the terror and brought in vast reinforcements, Jewish settlements illegally hoarded arms for self-defense. In towns everybody was on the alert. Some of my older classmates who had been to training camp on Mount Carmel joined Hagana and every now and then were absent from school for a day. The following morning, when the register was read out and a reason for their absence demanded, they gave the same brief answer: "I was busy."

It was a code phrase, indicating that they had been about on secret business. No teacher ever asked for details and no absentee was ever likely to volunteer any, but I knew that being "busy" meant either a day's drill somewhere in the hills or delivering coded messages to fully fledged members of Hagana.

On the surface, however, life went on as usual. Elegant women sat in open-air cafés sipping iced coffee, youngsters studied for exams, and the daily press carried advertisements inviting people to take their summer holidays abroad. The sea fare from Haifa to Athens was one Palestinian pound, then the equivalent of one pound sterling; sailing to Constanta, Brindisi, or Marseilles cost from two pounds upwards. Many went abroad and stayed away a long time to make the most of their holiday. My father too was on his travels again; he had taken a sabbatical and gone to the States to research and lecture. Before returning home he joined my brother in California and together they went on an extensive tour. They sent me a clipping from a local paper in Salt Lake City which carried father's photograph and described his style of delivery as "picturesque."

19

∼

Flare-up

IT WAS WINTER AGAIN. One blustering morning I arrived at school to find some classmates poring over a newspaper in a protected corner of the courtyard. I joined them to read a brief news item inconspicuously set on one of the back pages, reporting that a ship carrying "scalers" had been sighted off the coast of Haifa and intercepted by the coastal police.

"Scalers," in the sense of illegal immigrants, was a new word. One of the idiosyncrasies of the Hebrew language is to treat the Land of Israel as if it were the pinnacle of the universe. People wishing to settle in it can reach it only by walking upwards and are therefore no ordinary "immigrants" but "ascenders." "Ascenders," however, was not a strong enough word to describe those who had survived Nazi persecution, crossed the seas in dilapidated ships, and attempted to climb the steep road to the Land of Israel in spite of the British blockade. They were undaunted "scalers," *ma'apilim*.

As reports began sifting through about the true nature of the German labor camps in the hitherto unheard-of villages of Dachau and Buchenwald, helping "scalers" enter Palestine became a duty as morally unassailable as the Ten Commandments. Some illegal immigrants, to give them their official designation, were guided into the country through the Lebanon-Metulla border. The hundreds, and then the thousands, were transported to Palestine in ancient hulks acquired, refurbished, and put to sea by a secret network of dedicated patriots of whom we spoke only in whispers. It was January 1938 when I read that laconic news item about a dilapidated ship with a load of *ma'apilim* being arrested by the British coastal patrol. The following year such news items became more frequent. In March 1939 there were the *Artemis* and the *Sando*; in April there was the *Astia*. Then the *Assimi* came.

Its arrival was briefly reported in the evening edition of *Ha'aretz* on April 11: "At 10:30 last night," the report ran, "the coastal patrol detected a ship engaged in unloading people off the shores of Netanya. The ship attempted to escape but the patrol gave chase and opened machine gun fire. It is understood that there are several hundred men and women on board. Police boarded the ship and towed it to Haifa."

And there it was, in the beautiful new harbor in which I took such pride, visible to anyone looking down from Hadar Hacarmel or Mount Carmel, a decrepit object anchored among visiting British warships and regular passenger steamers. At first it was just the *ma'apilim* ship; two days after its arrest its name was given in the press as the *Assina*; three days later it became the *Assimini*; six days later it was finally identified as the *Assimi*.

By this time it was no longer on its own. In another corner of the harbor another illegal vessel was kept under guard. This one was known simply as the Yacht, since its original Greek name was as unpronounceable as it was unspellable. It had been towed in a couple of days earlier with some 170 refugees on board, many down with typhus and dysentery. As the small unseaworthy yacht was being disinfected by the health authorities, its human cargo was temporarily sardined into the *Assimi*. There were now nearly 450 men and women on board, fearfully waiting to hear whether they would be allowed to disembark into safety or sentenced to be deported towards death, as had the three other refugee ships caught earlier that year.

This time the leaders of the *yishuv* decided to take action. Action, in those early days of deportation, still meant verbal protest based on a peacetime notion that human life was precious. A desperate appeal was written on behalf of the boat people and published all over the country:

> We, the prisoners of the *Assimi*, survivors of concentration camps and Nazi persecution, are appealing to anybody with a human compassionate heart, to the entire civilized world, to the enlightened government of Great Britain: SAVE US.
>
> After weeks and months on the rough seas four hundred and thirty-five of us have been caught in two unseaworthy boats on the threshold of the only country left to us after all others had denied us help in our hour of need. We are sick and hungry: SAVE US.
>
> We now hear that we are to be sent back to sea, without lifeboats, without enough lifebelts, without enough bread and water. Whither shall we go? Are we to wander about the world doomed to die a slow and cruel death? And that under the auspices of Great Britain in the twentieth century? We appeal to the Jewish population, the people of Great Britain and the Palestine government: SAVE US.

In no other part of the country was the appeal so poignantly felt as in Haifa, where anybody who cared to look towards the harbor could discern the two vessels closely guarded by police boats. There was a flurry of activity. Women collected clothes and medicines; the leaders of the *yishuv* importuned the mandatory authorities; the mandatory authorities presumably consulted London.

Nearly two weeks passed in fear and hope. The Yacht's refugees had been returned to their disinfected bunks and on Saturday, April 22, both vessels were still clearly visible in the harbor, two floating prisons awaiting sentence. For most Haifaites that Saturday was the traditional day of rest. My sister and brother-in-law had come down to Bat Galim for the festive midday meal, and in the evening I put on my best frock and strolled towards the unfinished casino to meet friends. The center of the suburb was full of leisurely promenaders parading their new spring outfits and their dogs. Young lads flirted with young girls and I strutted about in my first high-heeled shoes feeling very glamorous, very desirable, and very self-conscious. By nine o'clock we were all indoors to observe the curfew. Haifa went to bed. Early next morning when I got to Hadar Hacarmel and looked down towards the harbor, the *Assimi* was no longer there.

The details of the deportation spread like wildfire. The order to deport had apparently been given a few days earlier but had been kept secret. Then, on Saturday night, as Haifa was asleep, police boats sailed towards the *Assimi* and loaded on a quantity of food and water calculated to last two days. The 270 refugees huddled together in the lower deck were not disturbed.

The police boats then motored to the other side of the harbor to load the same meager ration of water and provisions onto the Yacht, but since it was tiny and heavily overcrowded, it was impossible to put anything on deck without waking everybody up. General hysteria broke out. One hundred and seventy refugees, sick and feeble after their long ordeal, started screaming for help, rocking the boat, and trying to push the armed policemen back. The police fired warning shots in the air. The refugees put up their hands and cried out that they had nothing to lose, it made little difference whether they were killed by British bullets or died a slow death at the hands of the Nazis in Dachau and Buchenwald. While some began saying their prayers, others flung their clothes overboard and the few precious cans of water after them. The screams reverberated all over the port area. In the face of such suicidal frenzy the British officer in charge retreated and was ordered to put off deporting the Yacht until further notice. The *Assimi*, however, was towed out at daybreak and made to sail away.

At 6 A.M., as soon as the curfew was over, people who had heard the screams during the night began to converge on the port area to find out what it had been all about. When it was realized that the *Assimi* had been deported under cover of dark and that the Yacht was facing a similar fate, a general strike spontaneously broke out. Shops and businesses, just about to open, were shuttered down. Schools assembled their pupils at first bell only to dismiss them. The Technion students started a demonstration; women's organizations started another. All day long protest meetings were held at street corners and in the vast amphitheater. Telegrams of indignation were sent to Prime Minister Neville Chamberlain, Colonial Secretary Malcolm MacDonald, the Archbishop of Canterbury, President Roosevelt.

In the late afternoon some unusual activity was discerned in the harbor. Without binoculars it was difficult to tell what exactly was happening, but while several small vessels were slowly moving about, the Yacht appeared to be stationary. Suddenly everybody was saying that the 170 refugees had been allowed to disembark and were being driven to Bat Galim, where the Haifa Immigrants' Hostel was situated. Again the news spread like wildfire. When it was absolutely certain that the boat people were indeed on dry land, being housed, fed, tended, and comforted, there was a tremendous surge of triumph. Shops and cafés reopened for the few hours left before curfew, the streets were thronged with exuberant people, there were spontaneous outbursts of *Hatikva*, the Song of Hope.

The Yacht people were never deported. After some time in custody at the Immigrants' Hostel they were allowed to stay in Palestine and at long last start a new life. The dilapidated yacht was towed out of the harbor and left to the mercy of the sea. I kept seeing it for a long time, gradually shrinking in size as the waves tore it apart. One morning in mid July, some three months after it had first been sighted, it was no longer there. The last of the rotting wood had broken apart and what little there was had completely disintegrated, leaving no trace behind except some decomposed chips as light as cork.

I never learned what became of the *Assimi*; other ships took its place in the harbor, desperate little tubs with hundreds of refugees crammed into them. Following the precedent of the Yacht, the *ma'apilim* were now transferred to the Immigrants' Hostel at Bat Galim and later set free and allowed to stay in the country. It was a mixed blessing, for their numbers were carefully added up and deducted from the official quota. In July 1939 Colonial Secretary Malcolm MacDonald told the House of Commons that the quota had been exceeded to such an extent that in order to keep the balance sheet straight, no further immigration permits would be issued until the end of March 1940.

The deportation of the *Assimi* coincided almost to the day with the third anniversary of the Arab Revolt; but while the revolt was on the wane thanks to the tough measures taken by the British security forces, the thinking behind it had gathered a strong following among British politicians. The British government had withdrawn its support from the Peel partition plan and we now daily awaited the publication of yet another White Paper to learn what would become of us.

It came out on May 17, 1939, but the press was not allowed to publish it until the following morning. On the day, the people of Palestine were to be acquainted with the White Paper's recommendations through a live broadcast in the three official languages of the country: in Arabic at 8:00 P.M., in Hebrew at 8:15, and in English at 9:30.

On the evening of May 17 Haifa looked as it did a year earlier when a Toscanini concert was about to be broadcast. Again people huddled expectantly around radio sets in cafés and private homes and again we were anxious to pick up every single sound emanating from Jerusalem. Only the mood was somber; the tenor of the White Paper had been known for months and it was only a matter of hearing the grim details spelled out. At home mother fiddled impatiently with the knob and when all she got was a dry crackle she appealed to my superior technical skill to locate the station. I got nothing either. The Voice of Jerusalem was dead. The following morning we learned that a bomb had gone off at the Palace Hotel in Jerusalem, where the three studios of the Palestine Broadcasting Service were housed, at the very moment the White Paper was to be read on the air. It had been planted by a new patriotic group calling itself the National Military Organization or, in short, the Organization, *Irgun*.

And so it was left to the press after all to spell out the details of the new British policy on Palestine. They were worse, far worse, than our worst fears. Immigration was to be whittled down to a mere fraction and stop altogether in five years; our numbers were never to exceed one-third of the total population of the country; and in ten years' time, circumstances permitting, an independent state was to be set up based on majority rule, which meant Arab rule. The National Home was to be abandoned and young people like me, who had been born to freedom, were to become an unwanted minority in a hostile Arab state.

The reaction of the Jewish leadership to the White Paper was tantamount to a declaration of war on the mighty British Empire. "We are at war with this perfidious policy," ran the official statement. "We are at war with a regime founded on such a policy." Jewish Palestine went on a one-day strike. In Haifa 15,000 of us, nearly a third of the city's Jewish population, marched through the streets carrying such slogans as No Surrendar, United We Stand, and Down With the White Book, Our Only Book Is the Bible. Dozens of copies of the White Paper were publicly torn to pieces and flung in the air like so many dead doves of peace. When dark fell a huge white cardboard book was set on fire to the ominous chant of "No surrender." The curfew, only recently lifted, was reimposed.

Some two or three weeks later I happened to pick up a copy of the *Sunday Referee*, a London weekly long since discontinued, which carried on its front page an interview with George Bernard Shaw about his views on the White Paper. I was a great admirer of Bernard Shaw. I had already read *The Apple Cart* because it was required reading, *Saint Joan* because it was bound up in the same volume, *Man and Superman* because it was available at the school library, and an American anthology of Shavian witticisms entitled *Socialism for Millionaires* which I had found on the late Mrs. Haskell's bookshelves. I thought of Shaw as an Olympian, the shrewdest and wisest of them all, and was dumbfounded to read what he thought of the British promise to establish a Jewish National Home in ancient Zion:

> Of course the whole trouble arose through Balfour giving Palestine to Dr. Weizmann when it wasn't his to give. He might as well have handed him Madagascar.

Recalling that during the First World War Dr. Weizmann, then at the University of Manchester, made a discovery which helped the British war effort, GBS went on to give a playwright's account of an imaginary situation:

> The thing was that Dr. Weizmann had just supplied the British government with a cheap way of making cordite. Naturally, the government was very grateful, and Balfour said:
> "How much do you want?"
> "I don't want money," said Weizmann.
> "Quite so," said Balfour. "Then what shall it be? Baronetcy, earldom, or what?"
> "I don't want a title," said Weizmann. "I don't want anything for myself."

"You, a Jew, don't want anything for your-self!" said Balfour. "But you must want some-thing. What is it?"

Weizmann answered: "I want Jerusalem." And, since Jerusalem did not belong to Balfour, he was quite ready to balance the account by handing it over.

GBS ended by giving the British, the Arabs, and the Jews a piece of advice: "The British government can do little. They must leave the people of the country, Palestinian and Jew, to come to terms. If the inhabitants realize that it is up to them to do so, they will find a way out. For there is plenty of room for all of them."

For once the Shavian shrewdness was at fault and George Bernard Shaw's assessment of the Palestine triangle singularly ill-informed. As spring turned into summer the national turbulence increased. While Europe was nearing its own day of wrath, more and more refugee ships were leaving to seek haven in Palestine. The Immigrants' Hostel at Bat Galim, situated behind the shop where Mr. Milles was still selling his red sweets, had be-come too small to accommodate the growing flow of *ma'apilim*; nor were the authorities prepared to let them stay there any longer. In August a detention camp sur-rounded by barbed wire was built so that illegal immi-grants could be kept under close watch until they might be released against the small quota at some date in the distant future, or deported. That same month Haifa had its first blackout drill. Pulling black curtains over closed shutters in the stifling heat felt like putting up scenery for a school play. War was unreal. It only happened in history books.

The blackout drill was held on the night of August 28. On September 1 Hitler invaded Poland, and Britain and France gave him an ultimatum to withdraw or face war. Sep-tember 3, the deadline set in the ultimatum, was still a summer day, not as hot as the last two weeks in August, but pleasantly warm and caressing. I had dropped in on my sister and was admiring the view of the harbor from her penthouse balcony. It was as picturesque as ever, with the visiting British warships standing out in their whitish gray, the Italian and French passenger ships tantalizingly beckoning, the tugs, the cargo vessels, the small sea craft leisurely going about their mysterious business. Austria had been annexed, Czechoslovakia occupied, Poland invaded, yet there was Haifa, as peaceful and beautiful as ever in the warm sun, nestling confidently between the mountain and the sea. It was difficult to imagine it could ever be any different. When we turned on the radio to hear Neville Chamberlain's voice relayed from 10 Downing Street, we learned that Britain was at war. *We* were at war.

Two things happened almost simultaneously, and in the confusion of the day I could not make out which was more important. The first was that the German consul in Jerusalem was ordered to leave the country at once. Hundreds of people followed the police to see the representative of Hitler's regime being thrown out of Palestine; when the German flag with the swastika came down, the crowd cheered and booed and applauded. We were at war and that was our first little victory.

The second was a statement issued by the Jewish leadership, which read as follows:

The die is cast.

H. M. Government has today declared war on Hitler's Germany. At this time of emergency the Jewish population is expected to keep a threefold state of alert, for the defense of the homeland, the welfare of the Jewish people, and the victory of the British Empire.

The White Paper of May 1939 has hit us hard and we shall go on insisting on the right of the Jewish people to a homeland. But our opposition to the White Paper policy is not directed against England or the British Empire. The war which Nazi Germany has imposed on Great Britain is our own war. We readily offer the

British people and the British forces all the help we shall be able and allowed to give.

There was more to the statement than met the eye. Only a day before the declaration of war a *ma'apilim* ship called the *Tiger Hill* was intercepted off the coast of Tel Aviv and three of its unarmed refugees shot dead by British security forces. With reprisal in the air, the official Jewish leadership was not only professing its goodwill towards Britain but also urging the *yishuv* to show restraint at a time when the principle of retaliation was gaining ground. As air raid sirens were tested, public shelters prepared, and more refugee ships intercepted and denied haven, a new vow reverberated throughout the land: "We shall fight the war as if there was no White Paper and we shall fight the White Paper as if there was no war."

September continued warm and deceptively serene. In the evenings I stood on our tamarisk-surrounded balcony to watch the sun sink into the sea, straining my eyes to catch the precise moment when the flame-red horizon would begin to dim and change into melancholy gray. There was nothing to suggest that an era had come to an end, no omen to predict that the bitterest years in the history of the Mandate were about to begin.

20

Epilogue

GROWING UP has no visible finishing line. I cannot tell when I crossed it, but in retrospect I think that 1939 was perhaps the year when my leisurely ambling towards maturity quickened into conscious striding. There are, however, a few more recollections I would like to set down before bidding farewell to the Palestine of my childhood and adolescence.

For a while war continued to seem unreal. Blackout curtains, air raid shelters marked with an *S*, gas masks, and khaki uniforms were stage props ordered by remote statesmen directing a drama of speculation. When on July 15, 1940, the sirens sounded at 9:15 in the morning many of us thought it was just another drill. I was slow enough going to the shelter to catch a glimpse of ten aircraft flying in formation over the sea. Later the radio reported that anti-aircraft batteries positioned on Mount Carmel had driven off an Italian air raid on the port and the newly completed oil refineries in the bay. Two civilians had been killed.

On July 24 the air raid sirens again sounded at 9:15 A.M. Again ten Italian aircraft flew over in formation, again they missed their targets, and again they were driven off by anti-aircraft batteries; only this time they discharged their load over the town. Fifty civilians were killed, Jews and Arabs alike. After that there was no more dawdling, and running to the shelters with the first siren blast became routine, day and night. One evening an air raid caught me walking with a friend along a wild open stretch of Mount Carmel. The town below was blacked out and we watched the incendiary bombs drop in the dark like shooting stars, accompanied by the rumble of planes and the short bursts of anti-aircraft gunfire. When Italy surrendered to the Allies the air raids ceased.

In due course I went up to Jerusalem to study Arabic Language and Literature at the Hebrew University on Mount Scopus. At midterm a new student joined my literature class. She was an Arab girl, wearing a long shapeless dress and a veil which she never lifted. We sat in the same row, I on the extreme left by the window, she on the extreme right by the door. Every now and then I glanced surreptitiously in her direction to see how she was following the text through her veil and wondered at the courage and determination which had driven an Arab girl to overcome the traditional objections to higher education for women and brave the strangeness of a university, and an all-Jewish one at that. None of us ever spoke to her and she never spoke to any of us. After a while she ceased to attend.

Apart from a handful of students whose parents could afford to support them, the rest of us took whatever odd jobs were available in order to pay our way. A girl I knew, today a scientist at the Weizman Institute at Rehovot, worked as a waitress; my boyfriend for a few terms, then a student of Hebrew Literature and at the time of writing Israel's ambassador to Bonn, worked as a cinema usher. I started as a mother's help, went on to become a two-finger typist, and ended as a teacher at an evening school run by the Histadrut Trade Union for destitute children who worked during the day. Most of them came from oriental Jewish families who could hardly afford to feed their young, let alone send them to ordinary fee-paying schools. Some spent the daytime selling shoelaces and matchboxes in cafés, delivering groceries, or mopping floors; others loitered at street corners waiting for a chance to turn an honest piaster.

Classes were held on the premises of a large day school. We assembled at six o'clock and devoured, pupils and student-teachers alike, the hot meal provided by the Histadrut's social welfare department. Then we split up into our various classes, divided according to level of literacy rather than age. We taught for two hours five evenings a week, reading and writing, sums and, for the more advanced, English. One of my colleagues was a fellow student of Arabic Language and Literature, a pleasant-looking young fellow called Yitzhak, now President Navon.

In a country where education was not yet compulsory, attendance fluctuated from day to day. I often found myself going over the same ground every evening of the week, every time with a different group of pupils. As soon as I thought someone was making headway he or she would disappear without a word of warning. I was particularly disheartened by the defection of a girl named Bat Sheva who laundered clothes by day and had been making good progress in class. My inquiries among her friends were met with giggles.

"Didn't you know? She's got married."

She could not have been much over fourteen. A few evenings later she was waiting by the school gate looking as drab as ever in her working clothes. When she saw me she came up shyly and pressed something into my hand.

"That's for you."

It was a snapshot of herself, radiant in a richly embroidered oriental kaftan and headdress. On the back she had scribbled a touching thank-you message with only one spelling mistake.

Jews and Arabs did not mix socially but somehow I got to know a young Arab solicitor who took me to visit an evening school for Arab working children in Haifa's Old City. The faces staring at me in the bleak light of a bare schoolroom were just like those in my own classes in Jerusalem: the same dark hair and olive complexions, the same shrewd eyes, the same suspicious expression, the same nagging drive to acquire education which had been denied to them by poverty. They too spent the daytime delivering groceries or shining shoes, but there were no Bat Shevas among them. Education, such as it was, was only for boys. The teachers too were all male, young Arab intellectuals in immaculate European suits. As we talked about our respective schools and the need to abolish poverty and ignorance irrespective of creed I noticed the professional interest give way to a speculative leer; a Jewish girl venturing at night into the depths of the Arab Old City was surely a slut.

The war went on. There was no conscription in Palestine but the leaders of the *yishuv*, anxious for victory and hoping that active participation in the fighting would tip the scales in favor of an eventual Jewish state, prevailed upon the British government to allow Palestinian Jews to volunteer for the armed forces. The sight of the first Hebrew-speaking Jewish soldiers in British uniform made our hearts swell with pride. When women were later allowed to volunteer, they went into the British auxiliary services while civilians joined the Home Guard and first aid units. Identity cards were introduced. There was food rationing, blackout, and curfew; there were also secret training camps and arms drills. I had my first short story published.

I already knew that I was not cut out to be an oriental scholar, but English and French literature, which I wanted to study instead of Arabic, were taught in those days as subsidiary subjects only. I carried on indifferently, hoping to study abroad when the war was over. I left for London early in 1946, avid to see a world I had only read about, dreaming of a utopian postwar life purged of violence, prejudice, and misunderstanding.

Traveling to England began with an overnight train journey from Lydda Junction to Kantara in Egypt, continuing by ship through the Suez Canal and Port Said. I was tense and apprehensive. As my train was crossing the Sinai desert and gusts of sand were blowing in through a compartment window I had forgotten to close, I caught a glimpse of the evening sky, shot with rays of pink and orange. The sun was sinking into a sea of sand. Suddenly all was well. I thought of Perdita's words of comfort to Florizel when his father the king had forbidden their love:

> I was not much afear'd; for once or twice
> I was about to speak and tell him plainly,
> The self-same sun that shines upon his court
> Hides not his visage from our cottage, but
> Looks on alike. . . .

Yes, the sun looked on alike; on me, on others, on everybody. As long as it looked on, there was hope. There was always hope.

CUYAHOGA VALLEY CHRISTIAN ACADEMY
4687 WYOGA LAKE RD
CUYAHOGA FALLS, OH 44221
TEL. # 216-929-0575